JOURNEY

THROUGH

GENOCIDE

JOURNEY THROUGH GENOCIDE

Stories of Survivors and the Dead

Raffy Boudjikanian

DUNDURN
TORONTO

Cover Image: shutterstock.com/Mike Ver Sprill
All photo credits: Raffy Boudjikanian. Photo on page 111 unattributed.
Printer: Webcom

Library and Archives Canada Cataloguing in Publication

Boudjikanian, Raffy, author
    Journey through genocide : stories of survivors and the
dead / Raffy Boudjikanian.

Includes bibliographical references and index.
Issued in print and electronic formats.
ISBN 978-1-4597-4075-4 (softcover).--ISBN 978-1-4597-4076-1 (PDF).--
ISBN 978-1-4597-4077-8 (EPUB)

1. Boudjikanian, Raffy--Travel. 2. Genocide--Case studies.
3. Crimes against humanity--Case studies. I. Title.

HV6322.7.B68 2018   364.15'1   C2017-905721-9
                                             C2017-905722-7

1 2 3 4 5   22   21   20 19 18

We acknowledge the support of the **Canada Council for the Arts**, which last year invested $153 million to bring the arts to Canadians throughout the country, and the **Ontario Arts Council** for our publishing program. We also acknowledge the financial support of the **Government of Ontario**, through the **Ontario Book Publishing Tax Credit** and the **Ontario Media Development Corporation**, and the **Government of Canada**.

Nous remercions le **Conseil des arts du Canada** de son soutien. L'an dernier, le Conseil a investi 153 millions de dollars pour mettre de l'art dans la vie des Canadiennes et des Canadiens de tout le pays.

— *J. Kirk Howard, President*

VISIT US AT

dundurn.com | @dundurnpress | dundurnpress | dundurnpress

Dundurn
3 Church Street, Suite 500
Toronto, Ontario, Canada
M5E 1M2

To my great-grandfather Hovhanness Boudjikanian,
his son Armen, and genocide victims and survivors everywhere

Contents

Preface

All that follows in this book, except for the afterword, is based on my travel diary as kept during 2012. As such, some of the facts as they were at the time may have changed. This could apply to the numbers of Darfuri refugees as cited by authorities while I was in Chad, or the number of alleged génocidaires still hiding from the Rwandan government.

One of my interviewees in Turkey, Sarkis Seropyan, has since passed away. And the mayor of a district in Diyarbakir I mention in the epilogue has since become mayor of that entire city.

Since many of the genocide survivors and their families would be in danger if my contacts were identified as having shared their stories, some names have been changed.

An Introduction

When you are the descendant of genocide victims and survivors, *genocide* is not simply an abstract concept conjuring mental images of starving children or dead bodies in some faraway time and place. It is a constant reminder of what happened to your ancestors and the forces that shaped your life's path long before you first opened your eyes.

I was born in Beirut on May 8, 1984, around 10:00 a.m., if my mother's memory serves. Third child, second son, living with my family smack-dab in the middle of almost-daily bombardments and gunfire sweeping through the country caught in a civil war the U.N. estimates killed more than 120,000 people over its fifteen-year span.

When I was around four, I found out why I was born in Lebanon. One afternoon, I caught my father in our sunlit living room reading a big, black book, its cover decorated with skulls. That kind of imagery sticks in a child's mind.

"What's the book about?" I asked.

He explained, as much as a rational adult can explain, the concept of genocide to a small boy. He told me of the 1.5 million Armenians who were killed by Ottoman Turkish soldiers around 1915. My grandfather, barely older than me back then, escaped with most of his family from what is now known as eastern Turkey, what Armenians frequently refer to as historic Armenia, to Lebanon, to survive and start a new life. In comparison to many other Armenians, the Boudjikanians were lucky. My grandfather did lose his dad to the massacres, but he didn't endure the death marches through Syrian deserts that remain seared in my people's collective memory.

We'd be made to escape in my lifetime again, of course. This time, from a war-weary Lebanon to the safety of Canada.

The situations are parallel but not quite comparable. It was not a campaign of ethnic cleansing that made my parents decide one day that enough was enough and we'd be fleeing west, but the horrors of a country tearing itself apart. In fact, the strife had largely ceased by the time we did make the trip. Furthermore, our move was facilitated through a standard application for visas and waiting for an all-clear, rather than by means of a secretive escape. But, there you have it: my life's path was shaped by forces that were around long before I was.

* * *

If you include the tribes and kingdoms that would fight among each other and eventually merge, the Armenian civilization stretches back three millennia. Empires have risen and fallen around this small nation, sometimes swallowing it whole, sometimes carving it into smaller pieces among themselves; but it has endured and evolved, with its own history and customs. You're unlikely to discover much about it through any cursory research, though. Type the word *Armenian* into the world's most famous search engine, and there is a strong chance it will helpfully suggest *genocide* as a first-choice completion to your query.

You see, one entity that swallowed up much of Armenia for a long period of modern history was the Ottoman Empire, from the early parts of the sixteenth century until just about its own collapse in the first couple of decades of the twentieth.

By that point, a political party named the Committee for Union and Progress (CUP), also known as the Young Turks, had wrested control from the Empire's long line of sultans. The CUP was bent on seeing a version of Turkey for ethnically Turkish people from border to border. The Armenian nation was in their way, so the genocide was devised and carried out.

For the last century, Armenians have focused their public-relations efforts on pushing for international recognition of this crime against humanity, while the rest of our culture remains mostly a mystery to the world at large. Much of our unique literature is unread by a wider audience. Our famous authors are immortalized all over the modern country of Armenia in dramatic, Soviet-style statues, and their birth villages are sometimes rechristened in their names, but most of their writing is not translated into any other language. Our myths, arguably as compelling for schoolchildren as any about Hercules's twelve labours, are unfamiliar in other parts of the world, never having been adapted into serialized television or Hollywood mega-productions. Sure, you can visit Yerevan, Armenia's capital, and pose in front of a statue of David of Sassoon, the greatest of our mythical heroes. You can see him holding his Tour Gedzagi (The Sword of Lightning), astride his steed, Kourgig Tchalali, the legendary horse that could leap high as the sun in a single bound. But do not expect to find any plaque summarizing his tale at the public square in question.

Armenians who live in the country may get married in churches or monasteries with chapels nearly as old as the Christian religion itself; they may choose to have their children baptized in such structures, beautifully ornate buildings often nestled in picturesque mountainsides. But these, too, are not much advertised. One such monastery, Datev, is so high up a gorge that taking a rickety bus up the steep slope can feel like reaching for Heaven itself, especially on a foggy day. One slight slip-up by the driver can mean plummeting in the opposite direction instead. For those nervous about the bus ride, there is another option: a ride on the "Wings of Datev," the world's longest reversible cable car at 5,752 metres.

Another monastery, Keghart, is said to have housed both a piece of the lance that pierced the side of Jesus Christ and a fragment of Noah's ark. Carved in sheer volcanic rock, it is also home to a clear, clean stream of water rumoured to have healing capabilities.

We sing the praises of Armenian wine in our songs, but it is barely exported anywhere. The most popular Armenian brandy, Ararat, actually has "uncovering the past to understand the present" as one of its slogans, which, though just about abstract enough to remain obscure, surely reads more as an allusion to the genocide than to the idea of having a good time with your friends at a party.

As a non-Armenian, you're likely to experience "The Lecture," the story of the genocide, if you show any curiosity about Armenian culture at all to somebody of the background. Our capacity to kill the mood in a light-hearted conversation when anyone asks a couple of questions about our origins has become a bit of a joke, though it is not a very funny one.

If you consider that the heritage of this crime against humanity is what generations of schoolchildren have grown up with since, it's more sad than anything else.

Year after year, I've had teachers at my Armenian grade/high school set aside ample class time to go over this dark history, in increasingly greater detail as we children got older, and age restrictions fell away.

Then, there are the annual bus treks to Ottawa, for commemorations and protests before Parliament Hill. When I was a child, Canada hadn't yet acknowledged the massacres as genocide.

So, those Ottawa events served a dual purpose. They were calls to action for lawmakers in the Senate and House of Commons. They were also demonstrations directed at officials inside the Turkish Embassy, representatives of successive Turkish governments that denied the bloodshed of 1915 was planned and executed by the nascent Turkish state.

Nowadays, though Canadian recognition has come to pass through resolutions in the Senate and House of Commons and numerous declarations by the federal government, official Turkish denial shows no sign of abating, and therefore neither do the marches.

Many Armenians, I'm sure, have been questioned about spending so much time and energy seeking retribution for such a thing of the past. I've pondered the worth of it myself. After all, way before my time the world had already seen fresher horrors: the Ukrainian Holodomor, the Jewish Holocaust, the Cambodian genocide. As I was growing up, there was the Rwandan genocide, and then the war crimes in Kosovo. Just past the cusp of adulthood, I began to hear about Darfur.

Basically, the corpses have piled on and on, and there seems no shortage of genocides or massive massacres to rally against, so why stick to 1915?

In my case at least, that number, 1915, is a touchstone. It is what allows me to empathize with the pain and ordeal of genocide victims everywhere. It's not that by constantly speaking about the Armenian case I am forgetting all the others. The Armenian story is, on the contrary, my way of understanding them.

And, over the course of many years, I started to perceive the reverse must be true, as well. Meeting genocide survivors and hearing their tales first-hand would better illuminate what my ancestors went through, better allow me to picture where I'm from.

Obvious as that is in retrospect, it was not an immediate realization, but rather a truth that slowly dawned through my encountering different people and exposing myself to different stories.

I remember, duing my time as a university student, attending the screening of a fictional film depicting some of the Rwandan genocide and trembling in my seat as my mind swapped out Kigali for Turkey, and some of the victims depicted in the movie for my ancestors.

At that same screening, I met a young man who had survived the events, and interviewed him for a student publication. I bumped into him again on a subway station platform weeks later. He walked up to me, enveloped my hand in both of his, and, after making fun of me for getting his height wrong (I had unwittingly overestimated it by a couple of inches in my description), said, "Thank you for getting [my story] right."

It occurred to me then that, though Turkey's denial campaign may accentuate the importance of getting the story right for Armenians, we are not the only ones who find value in recording victims' traumas, and transmitting that record.

In the mid-aughts, Darfur in Sudan battled for foreign coverage space with ongoing wars in places such as Iraq and Afghanistan. Headlines trickling through captured my concern: were we again witnessing the same type of crime against humanity that killed and displaced my kin a century ago, the kind Rwandans were still reeling from?

What were the similarities among these different evils? What were the differences? Could speaking to survivors of some or all of them provide some hint about what we might do to reach that increasingly hollow-sounding goal of "never again"? Could that not at least help the world properly remember what happened to those survivors?

Trying to come up with answers, I started plotting a trip through all countries visited by genocide in the twentieth century, with the admittedly vague goal of linking them through a video or radio documentary, or newspaper articles (a book would not enter the equation until my travels were done). Soon, time and financial limitations reduced my scope to three destinations. Eastern Turkey would always be the end goal, given my personal connection. Rwanda stayed on my list because of its relatively unique status as a country where perpetrator and survivor now lived side by side in an uneasy peace. And I simply had to meet Darfuris who were still suffering from what had happened to them, still waiting for justice.

Experts and other journalists warned me that engaging the latter in their home country could place any witnesses I spoke to in peril. Perhaps, they said, I might get in and out of Sudan with no trouble to myself, and might obtain government permission to exit the capital, Khartoum, and enter Darfur, but I would no doubt be under tight supervision. And it was anybody's guess what would happen to any victim seen talking to me, after I left the premises.

I therefore switched Sudan for Chad on my itinerary. Hundreds of thousands of refugees had escaped from neighbouring Darfur, and would be more freely able to speak.

And so, this journey, after a little more than half a decade of having life and doubts get in the way.

Chapter 1

Preparations and Goodbyes

"This looks like it's been through a fire," the nurse in the travellers' health clinic snorts, holding the singed and blackened pages of my ancient vaccination booklet.

"It has," I reply with a grin, hoping she will inquire further, but she does not, perhaps deciding it is none of her business, perhaps deciding the conversation is too dark for a casual chat with a patient she doesn't know.

Answering her hypothetical follow-up questions on the paperwork would require delving into my birthplace, and delivering a short thesis about whether or not it is also "my home" or "where I'm from" — the type of debate that can keep many an immigrant up at night.

On October 13, 1990, that document had been tucked in a drawer in my parents' bedroom in Beirut. At the time, it held within its bright blue covers information pertaining to only the first six years and change of my existence. Like much else in that room, it did not escape unscathed from the bomb that exploded inside our third-floor apartment, shattering and scattering the glass doors to one of the two balconies.

Luckily, my parents, my sister, my brother, and I had already run downstairs into the building's underground shelter way before then. Earlier that morning, a fragment from another bomb had bored into our kitchen, cutting an almost perfectly circular hole through the wall. That had been enough of a hint: lingering in our home that day was a particularly bad idea.

We didn't find out about the fire the second bomb started in our building until the janitor burst into the concrete bunker late in the evening, warning us and our neighbours the low-rise had caught ablaze.

My dad recalls going on a recon tour, seeing the flames threatening our apartment, and returning downstairs to warn my mom. I recall the two of them deciding they needed to extinguish the fire before it spread anywhere else, and neighbours refusing to accompany them, fearing for their lives as the bombardments had barely ceased. I also recall myself and my siblings fearing for my parents' lives, and my sister in particular grumbling my parents were labouring under the illusion they were Mr. and Mrs. Superman.

I don't know who was watching over Mom and Dad that night, but they did manage to douse the fire. Later, once the sky stopped falling, we went upstairs ourselves. I quietly contemplated the soot covering their room and the adjacent hallway, darkening the bright walls, and I stared at the rubble covering our kitchen floor.

A lot in my parents' room burned that night, but the vaccination booklet pulled through. Somewhat worse for wear as the result of a few scorch marks, it nevertheless made the trip to Canada nearly a year later, along with our family.

*   *   *

Back at the Montreal travellers' health clinic, the story hovers untold on my lips, as the nurse carefully goes through all the precautions I would have to take for my upcoming trip to Chad, Rwanda, and Turkey: malaria pills every day in Africa, not eating any vegetables that I would not be washing myself with bottled water, shots, shots, shots … including one for yellow fever. The latter would come with a yellow certification paper to be folded and carried in my passport at all times, lest I be detained at a border following Rwanda.

* * *

It's departure day, and I'm at Trudeau International Airport, along with my parents, my brother, my sister, her husband, and their nearly two-year-old son.

Aren has actually said "Raffy" lately, my mom and his mom both insist. I have still not had the pleasure of hearing him say it myself.

Some people can go their whole lives without ever leaving their place of birth, and others cannot stand to be stationary while there is a whole world to explore. Aren will probably gravitate closer to the latter as he grows up. Already, he's been on a couple of trips with his parents, though he has not yet completed year two. He is born into a society where he is lucky enough to have such experiences.

As we all gather around an airport restaurant table, I can't shake the feeling I am about to meet a lot of people who do not have such fortune, and who likely never will. My first stops, after all, will be at refugee camps in eastern Chad, filled with Darfuri families who have barely escaped the genocide in their home country of Sudan. By late 2011, the Office of the United Nations High Commissioner for Refugees (UNHCR) estimated some 264,000 Darfuri refugees had fled Sudan for Chad.

We spend much of that last meal together trying to get Aren to say my name, but he seems equally as determined to keep his chubby baby mouth shut. Maybe it's because we won't let him play with the cutlery on the table, repeatedly moving it out of his grasp. At last, as we prepare to get up, he mutters "Ra-ffy," staring glumly into a pile of stale french fries on his plate.

The goodbyes are quick. The first ones, anyway. I hug everyone and march to the gates, where a security guard promptly reminds me of that cardinal twenty-first-century air-travel sin: carrying two canteens filled with water in the side pockets of my backpack.

I turn back to dump the liquid, taking advantage of the situation for a second round of goodbyes. My sister teases me about forgetting such a basic rule. My brother sums up everyone's sentiments quite succinctly: "Don't die!"

*   *   *

Night falls over Africa as our airplane prepares to touch down in N'Djamena, the capital of Chad.

This primarily Muslim country is considered a part of central Africa — after all, it runs on the multi-coloured Central African franc currency — but it is close to the continent's northeast. The former French colony has inherited Paris's mother tongue as an official language, though Arabic is just as common, and around a hundred more languages are spoken by its ethnically diverse population.

Chad is classified among the poorest countries by the United Nations Human Development Index; you can tell when the ones asking you for an extra franc are not only the unemployed, but people who have jobs.

And then there's the climate.

A passenger on my left, who has so far asserted his presence only by elbowing his way repeatedly through my personal space, decides to strike up a conversation on the temperature.

"I've been warned it's really hot," he says, palpable worry in his voice. His accent strikes me as African (as African as my Hollywood-trained ears can detect, anyway), which in turn, worries me. If someone from the continent (I believe he ended up revealing he was Tanzanian) is that concerned, should my own attitude toward what I have read on the matter of Chad's extreme heat be less flippant? And if he is so concerned, why is he arriving dressed in a full black suit, however sharp a figure it may allow him to cut?

"I've never been to Chad before," he continues.

"Me neither. But at least we're landing at night. How bad could it be?" I ask in a feeble attempt at reassurance.

My eyes follow his finger, tapping the screen in front of him, which displays in-flight information.

We're aboard our own Kourgig Tchalali, apparently, leaping high as the sun. At thousands of feet in the air, the temperature around us is already at twenty degrees Celsius.

I begin to share my fellow traveller's dread.

The numbers would change to thirty-seven degrees by the time we'd land. After 10:00 p.m.

Chapter 2

Planes, Paperwork, and Patience

"In my language, your name means future," I tell Abaka, my cab driver, staring at the dusty streets of N'Djamena through the cracks spread like a spider's web across his four-door's windshield.

He nods and curves his lips up weakly underneath his black, pencil-thin moustache. Dressed in flowing robes, like several of his fellow taxi drivers waiting for travellers in need of a lift, Abaka picked me up from the airport upon my landing, and brought me to a hotel he recommended, which I suspect netted him a commission.

Alone in standing above five storeys at the end of its dirt-road neighbourhood, the Chinese establishment Bei Fang looks over a relatively quiet block. Road traffic is scarce by day. By night, huddled masses of homeless gather around smaller buildings across the street.

The hotel boasts a courteous staff, but places me in a third-floor room with a frequently malfunctioning AC unit, and charges like a veritable Best Western or Marriott for levels of service comparable to a bad youth hostel. The Wi-Fi has no reach beyond the main floor, though there's some comfort there as I can freely lounge around a large conference room that is clearly meant for some sort of business-class clientele but remains mostly vacant throughout my stay; the TV displays a handful of channels in Arabic only, a language I do not speak or understand; and the proximity of the toilet bowl to the unenclosed shower in my cramped bathroom means I have to remember to move the toilet paper out of the water's range before deciding to freshen up.

It is better than the alternative: an online reservation I'd made at a hotel, which to this day I'm not sure exists, as calling it to confirm anything never yielded any results. I admit, though, that relying on a random stranger to safely bring me to a place to spend the night in the middle of a country where I did not know anyone was not the finest of contingency plans. In fact, during that original talk with Abaka, I fleetingly recall imagining that getting into the car of a stranger here was a fine way for a Westerner to get kidnapped. But the pickup area in front of the airport felt like an unlikely place to pull off such a stunt. Either that, or fatigue won out over paranoia.

He is a quiet fellow, Abaka. Our minimal, utilitarian conversations occur in French, and he does not say much other than thanks, good morning, good afternoon, and when am I picking you up next.

On one occasion, as he dropped me off back at the Bei Fang around noon, I attempted more small talk. "So I guess you'll continue working now, huh?"

"It's too hot to work this time of day," he said drily. "I'm going to go take a nap until around four."

Even if the heat hadn't been so overwhelming, N'Djamena was not the kind of place where a foreigner like me could run errands by walking, or by hopping on a bus. I just wouldn't be spending enough time there to become accustomed to its sprawled dirt roads.

And forget renting a car. I never asked Abaka about the aforementioned windshield, but five minutes spent on any street in the city would be enough for mostly anyone to fill in the blanks. Drivers honk incessantly, cut through lanes without signalling their intentions, and regularly miss each other by a few inches, as pedestrians do their best to stay out of the way. I'm reminded of my native Beirut, or Rome, or Yerevan just after the new millennium.

It's not just the transportation in N'Djamena that can be overwhelming for a visitor. Taking pictures or filming is forbidden, unless you have explicit written permission by authorities. You could make some attempt at sneakiness about it, but the police/army-to-tourist ratio means you wouldn't exactly be playing the odds.

None among the handful of other guests I see at the Bei Fang on evenings appear to be tourists. There's certainly not a camera flash in sight, and the language barrier makes it difficult to befriend them.

Sitting down at a table at Bei Fang's ground-floor reception hall, I banter with a handful of Egyptian guests while munching away at a dinner plate that has way too much meat and no greens on it at all. Of course, it's not that the presence of the latter would make a difference anyway, since I have strict instructions from the travellers' health clinic nurse not to eat vegetables I have not washed myself. To my surprise, the men ask the hotel's manager, who seems eager to please her customers, to provide the reception hall's wall-mounted flat-screen TV with access to a channel they'd really like to watch: the CBC.

It feels completely extraordinary, downright wonderful to me, that Africans are familiar with my employer, Canada's public broadcaster, when I've sometimes found myself having to explain its existence in the country's mostly francophone province of Quebec as the "English-language version of Radio-Canada." On a couple of occasions, I've had to actually clarify I'm not from the news agency branch of a certain major Canadian bank with an acronym the CBC is just one letter shy of. Beaming with pride, I tell the Egyptians I work there back home. They're delighted at first, then puzzled at finding out I don't speak Arabic.

When our enterprising hotel staff successfully fulfills their request on the next evening, I see the root of the confusion: theirs is not the CBC at all, but the cbc, the Capital Broadcasting Center, an Egyptian entity that shares the three letters of its call sign, but not their case, and little else with the Canadian organization.

*   *   *

Armed police and men in army fatigues patrol most of N'Djamena, and wall-sized posters of President Idriss Déby also keep watch over the populace. No ignoring the cliff's edge here; Chad precariously balanced on it in 2008, with Déby's troops barely able to crush a rebellious uprising. Opposition forces reached the capital, and were pushed back only thanks to assistance from the French army. Now the country's government is more like a rock climber after a slip, trying to clamber back over the brink.

The atmosphere this creates does not exactly scream travel-friendly, and it was indeed a rarity for me to encounter anybody coming to Chad for anything other than work reasons.

If you are a foreigner here, there's a good chance the business you're visiting on has to do with the UNHCR.

It runs several camps on the rim of the Sahara Desert, near the country's eastern border with Sudan, hosting people who have escaped Darfur.

So far, the UNHCR had proven fairly accommodating, indicating in preliminary communications before I left Montreal that I would have a chance to visit two different refugee camps: Goz Beïda and Farchana. Still to be settled was the matter of a translator. I'd need one, as most of the refugees would be unlikely to speak English or French.

*   *   *

Abaka drives me to my first meeting with UNHCR officials in the Chadian capital, to further set up the trips to the camps.

The compound itself reinforces the point that N'Djamena is no picnic. The container units carved out into air-conditioned offices hunker down behind barbed wires, concrete walls, guards, and metal gates. I can get in through security only after exchanging my journalistic ID for a day-visitor's pass. An irrational part of me fears I'll never see my journalist ID again.

My contact is as friendly in person as he's been through emails and over the phone prior to my flight. We easily mix French and English, a practice I'd assumed I'd leave behind in Montreal, as he explains that I should be able to stay at Goz Beïda for just under a week, and about the same amount of time in Farchana.

That should allow me, I thought, to interview a number of genocide survivors before flying to Rwanda, my next destination. My trips within Chad will be done by plane, too. Some nine hundred kilometres separate N'Djamena from Goz Beïda, the further of the two camps. With normal road infrastructure, you could drive there in about a day; but there's no such animal in much of this country, and so the UNHCR plans to arrange me a seat on a U.N. World Food Programme flight. Quicker and safer, I'm told, than days of driving through blinding heat.

Recovering my press pass with ease (and shame about my earlier misgiving about ever seeing it again), I move on to my next errand, dealing with Chad's one major inheritance from France besides *la Langue de Molière*: onerous bureaucracy.

As well as requiring travellers to fork over a hundred dollars weeks in advance of their trip to get a visa stamped onto their passports, Chadian authorities also insist you visit a local police station upon your arrival.

There, you must earn a further couple of colourful stamps on your passport by, among other things, filling out two forms so obsessed with obscure life details I'm surprised Facebook hasn't bought the rights to use them.

Abaka waits outside for me again. As I walk into the station's courtyard, I hear a new nickname given me by a curious local patrolman, a name that emphasizes just how rarely foreigners visit Chad. "*Monsieur le blanc*," ("Mr. Whitey," roughly, in English), he baptizes me with a laugh, then points me to a small administrative building.

Inside, the lights are off and the door open, an almost futile countermeasure to the stifling heat.

A bored receptionist watches as I scribble my name, the name of my father, the name and maiden name of my mother, my date of birth, place of birth (you know, some of the stuff that's already on my passport, which was already stamped with a visa), original nationality, current nationality (it falls short of asking for a future nationality), marital status, religion, denomination, etc.

Occasionally, the worker suggests a mild interest in the data. "Ah you're originally Lebanese," she remarks, looking at the form. "But your passport is Canadian." Funnily enough, the one-third of my identity that's the main catalyst behind the trip is the only personal detail about me that is not recorded on the paperwork, and therefore does not attract her attention either. She does not receive The Lecture.

It is all mildly irritating, but could be much worse. My guidebook issues a warning here for travellers: prepare to pay an extra bribe if you want this bureaucratic adventure to proceed smoothly. In my case, either a UNHCR letter stating I'm a journalist on business, or just plain luck, means I avoid that particular annoyance, for now.

* * *

In my next meeting with the UNHCR, the organization puts me in touch with a translator — one they assure is no stranger to the camps.

And I meet him a day later, at UNHCR headquarters. White prayer robes flow about the tall, lanky Chadian, who, reserved and formal, says little during our brief encounter beyond extending his long fingers for a vigorous handshake.

I return to the hotel and ask the manager if 5:00 a.m. is too early to expect breakfast, telling her I would like to leave the place by 6:00 a.m., since my flight the next morning is at 8:00 a.m.

She laughs, says there is no way the plane will take off that early. I tell her it's a U.N. flight and I've been assured the schedule is accurate.

She laughs again and nods, more of an "If you say so" than a "Yes."

The two boiled eggs and toast sit in my gut uncomfortably while I pace back and forth in Hassan Djamous, N'Djamena's practically deserted airport. The two-floor structure stretches like an overgrown shoebox, with check-in, security, and a single departure lounge occupying ground level, and a couple of lonely cafés above the stairs.

It takes about half an hour for my translator to show up, now looking way more relaxed in a checkered shirt and khaki pants. For a while I watch, amazed, at how easily he mingles with both staff and passengers, popular as a varsity football player on a college campus. He elucidates the mystery by explaining he used to work here.

Around this time we receive a first announcement of a flight delay, due to low visibility. I'm no aviation expert, but I've definitely taken off in cloudier skies.

"When do you think we'll leave?" I ask my translator, surprised to see I seem to be the only one overly concerned about being late.

He shrugs, says maybe 10:00 a.m., maybe not. "Look at them, you couldn't even tell they're travelling," he adds, as we take in the indifference pervading among other passengers.

Deciding I need coffee, I ask him if he wants to venture upstairs with me, but he declines.

I walk to one of the cafés, where the cashier appears irritated, more than anything else, to have to serve a customer. Or maybe she was supposed to catch the flight. Who knows?

My order arrives as a mug with a satchel of what is supposedly caffeine ("MacCoffee" it is helpfully labelled, suggesting the manufacturer's fondness for either fast-food chains or anti-virus software), four sugar cubes (!), and a thermos, all slid over with a certain curtness, and I assemble my drink.

I first sip the coffee with only two of four sugar cubes. After my first taste, I throw the remainder in and finish my beverage.

I go back downstairs, and more waiting ensues, until at last, at noon, we are informed the sky's simply too foggy for takeoff today and we'll have to return the next morning.

Again, most passengers are not bothered by this, some laughing as they leave the airport. When agreeing to a new meeting time with my interpreter, I show I am puzzled. He says people are just used to it.

Bei Fang's manager, evidently, is also used to righteous patrons humbly returning to her expensive rooms after boasting, cocksure, about their flight schedules. However, she's nice enough not to say "I told you so."

*   *   *

Day two arrives. And, once more, 8:00 a.m. becomes 10:00 a.m., and 10:00 a.m. becomes noon. This time, we're told the pilot is sick and therefore the plane won't fly today. Furthermore, tomorrow is Sunday, and there is no plane. We'll have to wait for the start of a new week for takeoff.

The pilot. Sick.

Tired of Bei Fang's exorbitant prices, and too proud to admit defeat a second time, I follow a hotel recommendation from my guidebook and get myself to Big Cosmo Guest House. My ground-floor room is a little cooler. Though it has no AC, it does have an electric fan that actually works — and it's half the price of my first stay. The TV has a couple of French-language channels, but a reception problem means there's so much white noise that it's impossible to actually watch anything. The food, too, is better, and served in a lively courtyard restaurant.

I slowly pick away at my evening chicken meal, the salad dutifully pushed to a side of my plate untouched, following the travel health clinic nurse's advice. Nearby, a charcoal and burnt-orange lizard cools itself on the stone floor, ducking away from the sun in the shade of creaky deck furniture. The common agama, as the sub-Saharan native species is known, is famous for the "pushups" (really the bobbing of its head and upper body up and down) it performs during mating season to woo females. But, in this heat, any such demonstration of physical fortitude is not to be hoped for. Besides, its gender is hardly clear to a layperson like me and there are no others of its kind to be seen. Lack of picture-taking permissions notwithstanding (the UNHCR arranged them for me, but exclusively for my stay at the refugee camps), I discreetly snap a couple of photos with my smartphone.

No, the camera police don't notice, but my waiter does.

"That's a very nice phone," he says.

I thank him, but that's not what he's getting at.

"Can I have it?" he asks.

Awkwardly, I tell him I don't have another, and need this one for work.

*   *   *

Day three arrives, and brings with it the standard couple of hours' delay. Again I amble around the airport.

A man sitting legs akimbo in a white robe underneath a pillar takes notice of me, chortles, and looks up. Clearly he's been paying attention to my schedule.

"Hahaha, how are you? How are you?" he asks, with a familiar, repetitive lilt that suggests we must have greeted each other on the two previous days.

"You're here every day you, aren't you? You're here every day," he chuckles, and looks away.

Ha, hilarious.

We take off at last. On the fifty-person propeller plane I occupy a window seat adjacent to the emergency exit. It is April 23, 2012. Beneath me and the soft white clouds unrolls the brown, dry land of Chad. I dream it is almost exactly ninety-seven years ago, and I'm observing a different desert landscape — seeing the endless rows upon rows of Armenians walking, crawling, and falling through Syria's Der El Zor in the death marches organized by the Turkish regime.

*　*　*

For the first time in my life, I'm about to meet large groups of women and men who suffered ordeals similar to those of my people's ancestors, though under different circumstances. The Darfur divide between perpetrator and victim has played out along race and resource lines. There's been no religious aspect to the clash: the majority of both victims and assailants are Muslim.

The Fur, Zaghawa, Masalit, and other black tribes settled in villages in north Darfur have been hunted down and slaughtered by the Janjaweed, brutally efficient horsemen mercenaries backed by Sudan's Arab government. Underlying tensions between those tribes and the more nomadic Arabs in south Darfur were heightened by years of drought beginning in the '80s: the region's once-fertile lands are no longer able to accommodate everyone.

In the midst of all this, two rebel groups, the Justice and Equality Movement (JEM) and the Sudan Liberation Army

(SLA), rose up against the Sudanese government. The government pushed back, turning its forces against not just those two groups, but also against the settled tribes, viewing them, as the International Criminal Court reported in its ruling on the fighting, as "being close to the SLM/A, the JEM and other armed groups opposing the Government of Sudan in the ongoing armed conflict in Darfur." Along with its own forces, the government also enlisted the Janjaweed in its battles against the rebel groups and in its campaign on the unarmed black population in the north of the country.

In a parallel development, the Sudanese government had also been clashing with rebels in the south of country.

In 2009, an arrest warrant was issued for Sudanese president Omar al-Bashir for crimes against humanity by the International Criminal Court as a result of his regime's actions in Darfur. A second arrest warrant specifically added genocide to his charges a year later, but little has come of the paperwork other than hand-wringing over who may try to act on it.

* * *

As I contemplate meeting some of the refugees, I ask myself what the escapees will be like. Will they look me in the eye? Will they share their stories of hardship? Do I deserve their attention? I try blocking out the questions by focusing on the emergency exit directions written in English on the door next to me. My ability to speak and read the Bard's language — divined by the flight attendant thanks to the "Nova Scotia" stitched in white on my navy-blue baseball cap — has earned me this particular seat.

In case of a forced landing, I am to open the door, step outside, and point fellow passengers to the rear of the plane as they leave, making sure they avoid running toward the propellers. For extra insurance, I am to place myself between the propellers and said exiting passengers.

Be as multilingual as possible, they said. It'll only open doors. Nope. It'll make sure you open the doors, and offer yourself up as sacrifice to the roaring propellers.

I arrive at Goz Beïda in the evening, after a layover in Abbéché, a hub city where many Chadians change flights.

My stay at the camp is brief, due to the previous holdups. I'm greeted by Chadians who work for the UNHCR. The head of Goz Beïda voices his regret at the delays and has me installed inside my once-cargo-container-now-room for the night. Its hollow floor beats like a drum as I walk across, and the bathroom engages in a veritable new-age concerto when I flush, but there is suitable distance between the toilet bowl and the shower. More importantly, there is smooth Wi-Fi, and, most importantly, there is functional air conditioning.

My translator, who joined me on the flight, disappears with ease into the local town of Goz Beïda, not too far from the compound. I'm a little alarmed he'd just walk away from the safety of the thick walls guarding the U.N. site, but his nonchalant demeanor reminds me he's done this before. He asks me to text him if I need anything.

Administrators arrange a quick tour of the area for me aboard a white UNHCR-marked Jeep. I'm accompanied by a young man from N'Djamena who seems pleased to answer my questions. Unlike many people I'll meet in Chad, he speaks English happily. I sense he relishes the chance to ditch French and practise the other empire's tongue.

Goz Beïda's UNHCR field office coordinates two refugee camps: Djabal and Goz Amer. Between the two of them, they

In my first encounter with genocide survivors on the trip, I quietly observe a group of them playing soccer at sunset in Goz Beïda, Chad.

house nearly forty-four thousand refugees. It's a pity I won't be able to meet more of them, tucked away as they are behind their mud-walled huts or off on trips into the bush to collect firewood, but my visit is short, and there's only so much I can accomplish.

On our drive in the Jeep, I text my interpreter to see if he can pop back out, on the off-chance some refugees would be willing to be interviewed this evening, but he replies he's just found a place to stay and wants to rest up for the night.

It turned out to be just as well, for I don't really get to interview anyone when I meet them. In my mind, I'd built up this first encounter as a dramatic sit-down where members of this grieving community would tell their harrowing tales of woe. Instead, to my great astonishment, I discover children who wave and laugh when they see the white UNHCR vehicle and are further amused when I take out my audio recorder and still camera.

The sun sets over a group of them playing soccer, kicking up pink puffy clouds of sand as they run after the ball. I find no visual distinction between the two teams. There are skins and shirts on both sides. A couple of donkeys solemnly cut a path through the players, but they don't seem to mind.

I watch the kids, how happy they appear, and muse on whether or not my grandfather managed to smile so widely after he first escaped to Lebanon from eastern Turkey, leaving his dad behind.

* * *

On my only evening in Goz Beïda, I eat dinner at the container that serves as a kitchen and cafeteria for staffers of the UNHCR and other humanitarian organizations. Over beef curry and basmati rice prepared by U.N. cooks, I meet a couple of workers from GIZ (the Deutsche Gesellschaft für Internationale Zusammenarbeit, or German Society for International Co-operation), and a German NGO that works with the country's government to meet its foreign aid objectives. GIZ specializes in sustainable development.

One of the workers informs me there's beer to spare for drinking and we split a can. He and his colleague listen with interest to the purpose of my trip. It turns out they have been on missions through many African countries: from Mali to the Ivory Coast.

When two of us step outside into the cool desert air after we finish eating, I'm surprised at how much more agreeable the weather has become. The worker shrugs, explains it's obvious I've never been to a desert before, his eyes beaming with mischief through thick glasses and over a thin smile framed by his ginger moustache.

I ask him what is the most pressing environmental issue in Chad's refugee camps. He points to the surrounding emptiness: barely any trees to be seen. The influx of hundreds of thousands of Darfuris into an already resource-poor region has created tensions between the Sudanese and local Chadians.

Darfuris escaped here from their home, running away from those who'd kill them over land. They're safer now, but it seems peace with neighbours over who has the right to use what remains an elusive goal.

The GIZ workers wish me good night and take their leave.

Chapter 3

Victims of the Janjaweed

Historians commonly acknowledge the Armenian genocide started on April 24, 1915, when Ottoman authorities imprisoned some two hundred intellectual leaders of the community in Istanbul, most of them later executed.

On the ninety-seventh anniversary of that date, I fly from one camp housing Sudanese refugees, Goz Beïda, to the next. Farchana, with twenty-three thousand refugees, is a slightly smaller camp, and I'll be staying there longer.

South of Goz Beïda and a little closer to N'Djamena, Farchana is not too far from the Sudanese border. I cannot help pondering that one of the worst humanitarian crises of our times lies a mere seventy kilometres further east. Many journalists have made it, sneaking between the two countries by night.

Doing that, though, wouldn't be easy. As in Goz Beïda, the U.N. compound proper in Farchana sits behind reinforced concrete walls, and officials strictly impose a 6:00 p.m. to 6:00 a.m. curfew for any humanitarian organization workers and guests. Farchana village, which is inhabited by local Chadians, is a short drive from the structure.

The Farchana refugee camp in eastern Chad, which houses Darfuri escapees from the genocide in neighbouring Sudan, their home country.

The two places are separated by a *wadi*, a deep, sandy trench I'm told turns into a river during the country's rainy season. When the UNHCR delegation points this out, all I see are a couple of dried-up trees jutting out of the ground, and docile donkeys strutting nearby.

Upon our arrival at the compound, I'm again given a container by the UNHCR: bed, washroom, a desk that would soon find itself covered by bottles of water, Wi-Fi connection ... and, once more, thankfully, functional air conditioning.

My translator and I are introduced to Marcel Raad, head of security. The thirty-nine-year-old wears sunglasses, a baseball cap, and a short-sleeved shirt — all typical of aid worker apparel — but his square jaw and shoulders could easily be poured into some presidential secret service security detail's suit instead.

"You're from Lebanon," Marcel immediately says, perhaps finding something in my French accent that gives it away.

The Farchana refugee camp in eastern Chad. We would never leave a UNHCR site without the company of a security convoy.

Only later do I consider he must have seen the photocopies of my Canadian passport, which shows my place of birth, since his colleagues in Ottawa and N'Djamena asked to reproduce the travel document.

Of the three identities that bounce around in my head, the Lebanese tends to be the most possessive. Many Lebanese will insist I present myself as such once they find out I was born there, and are mock-dismayed when they discover I've long forgotten what little knowledge of Arabic I possessed as a child. No amount of sincere apologizing grants me forgiveness. Canadians, typically, at some point after making acquaintance will politely inquire about my ethnic origin if they cannot take a guess. For other Armenians, of course, it's obvious as soon as they hear my full name. Between the "Raffy" we seem to have appropriated from its Persian roots and claimed for ourselves, and the telltale "ian" suffix dangling at the end of what's already a mouth-ful of a last name, it's not exactly what you'd call a mystery.

Marcel, half-Lebanese himself, doesn't try testing my Arabic, so I am spared the awkward mea culpa.

Marcel takes us to his office where we receive a security brief-ing about the site. As in a '40s film noir, the sun rakes the shadows of his half-shut window blinds through the small desk space. His tone and the PowerPoint presentation make it pretty clear: this is serious business. And he reinforces the impression by explaining the compound was held up by bandits little more than three weeks ago. They simply leapt over the perimeter wall and pointed a gun at a U.N. employee, forcing guards to co-operate. "They just got away with around €300," Raad says, "along with a couple of sunglasses."

I suppose incidents like this explain the curfew.

The briefing over, my translator leaves to find sleeping arrange-ments at Farchana village. Seeing the difference between the two places is difficult, arguably impossible, without the telltale signs belonging to non-governmental organizations at the camp. Both Farchanas consist mostly of mud-walled huts with straw roofs.

The region's poverty strikes all the harder when Marcel Raad takes me for a visit to the village's local authority — a prefect whom etiquette obliges me to meet before I may conduct any interviews.

His house is as simple an affair as any of the surrounding huts, if somewhat larger. Our meeting room is practically spar-tan; the earth at our feet free of covering.

After being introduced to the prefect, I sit quietly and listen to the circle of men speaking. The meeting has an air of informal-ity: there is no written agenda whatsoever, though it's clear the subject is the day-to-day affairs at the camp.

The question of money comes up; particular mention is made of the need to assist the thinly budgeted DIS (Détachement

Intégré de Sécurité), the Chadian forces in charge of security at the UNHCR. "Maybe our Canadian friend can help us," the prefect jokes, laughing through his goatee.

My mind flashes back to N'Djamena's presidential head-quarters, occupying entire city blocks, which Abaka drove me past on an errand. Beautiful bronze statues of freed slaves watched over a central square, so tall the tips of their heads were visible from the balcony near my room in Bei Fang. Erected in 2010 for the fiftieth anniversary of Chad's independence, the monument cost millions in U.S. dollars, all public money. This while people sleep in mud huts.

But I chuckle awkwardly at the prefect's suggestion and say nothing else.

On the next day I'm taken to the refugee camp proper, in the usual convoy of white and green UNHCR and DIS vehicles. The beginning of the arranged visit is surprisingly formal. I'm led into a "therapy centre," a meeting room in a building that reminds me of a church hall. We walk through a hole in the shape of a door. The desert sunlight seeps in from the rectangle of nothing and the square windows, its harshness muted by the yellow walls.

A large group of refugees from both Farchana and neighbouring camps occupies wooden benches set atop the blue-carpeted floor. A representative from a refugee welcoming committee installs me and my interpreter at a table at one end of the room, facing them, next to Marcel Raad and other repre-sentatives from various non-governmental organizations.

The rep starts introductions, but I'm uncomfortable. Sitting at the table puts my microphone out of range and means I will be unable to properly record audio during interviews. Besides, I'm not sure these genocide survivors would appreciate my asking them questions from several feet away, like some sort of terrible musical talent show host. It's bad enough the survivors from my first encounter remained distant, almost mirage-like on their soccer field; I do not wish to reproduce the effect for the second meeting.

On the other hand … could demanding to sit closer to the people I'll be speaking to be some sort of taboo? That's never come up in any literature I've read about Darfuris.

"I can't work like this," I at last work up the gumption to tell Marcel. He solves the problem immediately by explaining to the committee rep that my translator and I need to move over to be able to listen properly to the refugees.

And boy, do they have a lot to say.

* * *

Hassan Mohammad stares intensely as he explains how he escaped from Madeine, his home village in Darfur, nearly a decade ago. In a beige shirt with matching pants, he is among my first interviewees of the day. My interpreter on my right translates the long, Arabic sentences that Mohammad mutters under his moustache.

Some of his story will soon become so familiar as to turn bits and pieces of the translations superfluous. "Janjaweed," the key word, designating the Sudanese government-backed militia that carried out much of their dirty work, is on Mohammad's lips — and will be on those of many of his kin.

Mohammad says the Janjaweed made a habit of blocking people's paths when they returned from buying goods and produce at local markets. If you raised your hands, he says, they would maybe let you live. But some would try to escape.

"Sometimes kids waiting for food at home are told their father is dead. Sometimes, people get to return, empty-handed," he says through my translator.

"And so you and your family decided to escape. In 2003 … ?" I prompt.

The breaking point for Mohammad's clan, it turns out, was a day they saw a neighbouring village set ablaze. Deciding they had to dash home to pick up supplies for the road, they left four families sheltered underneath a tree.

"But when they returned," my translator says, "those people were already dead."

"You … you saw them dead yourself?" I ask.

In his long, winding response, Mohammad points his index finger at one of his eyes. I wait for the translation, but presume that means an affirmative answer to my question.

When it comes at last, the reply is much more devastating. "Some of them died in front of me," Mohammad says. "And I buried them myself."

Rida Abbas is from the village of Jennena in Darfur. Hers also is a tale of Janjaweed, stolen goods, and flight, its horror in sharp contrast with her beautiful white veiled dress and its purple, black, and yellow flower prints.

She was luckier than Mohammad. Janjaweed shot her daughter in the leg before the two could make their escape, but the girl survived. Nine years later, though, she still limps, an amputee.

A baby mumbles softly in the circle of people behind us as I continue my interviews. He is happy, giggling as he manipulates a flip-top cellphone's buttons and bathes in the glow of its monochrome screen. I'm reminded of my nephew, who displays a similar fascination with handheld devices, but doesn't look underfed.

Insects flutter on Faridah Badawi's sandalled toes as she tells her tale. She, a Zaghawa, is from a village of the same name in Darfur. Again, I hear of Janjaweed, and the year 2003.

On a September afternoon, Badawi, then thirty-five, was feeling sick, and her father told her to wait at home while he went to fetch medicine at the Arba Mouli public market.

About an hour after his departure, at 2:00 p.m., Badawi started hearing noises. "There were gunshots, light artillery, heavy artillery," she explains in short, staccato sentences, punctuated by pauses.

"Masses were dispersed, people were screaming." In a panic, the ailing Badawi ran out of her house and toward the market herself.

Sure enough, the Janjaweed had already done their work when she arrived. "My dad was among those who had been killed," she says.

Meanwhile, both Zaghawa village and another adjacent town were attacked as well.

Badawi recalls more than ten people dead that day in total, and says none of the victims could receive the dignity of individual burial. "It would have taken too long," she says, many people being afraid their tormentors could return.

They dug graves each large enough to hold three or four of the dead.

As if their faith in the government had not been tested enough, "authorities arrived, observed what had happened, but didn't do anything about it," Badawi says.

She lost two other members of her clan, too, in the same incident … and as the Janjaweed visits multiplied, so did the murders and rapes.

At last, Badawi and her village fled, along with neighbouring people. They escaped by splitting into groups of few more than ten, each waiting until nightfall before making their move.

Badawi lives in relative safety now in Farchana, but her heart ever looks at beloved Darfur. She has not heard of her older brother since leaving her home country. "I do not know if he is dead or alive," she says.

And there is another reason, too, she is constantly turned toward Sudan. She misses it. "As long as [Sudanese] President [Omar] al-Bashir has not resigned or left, I cannot go back," she says, "but I do wish to return to my village, one day."

Some resisted escape longer than others. Zayd Hasid Waleed is now a teacher at a refugee camp, but lived in a village called Azerné in Darfur's Kanaré region as a farmer. He remembers his troubles beginning earlier than those of most, in 1997. Returning from religious school, Waleed, a teenager at the time, found his home burning to the ground, along with the rest of Azerné.

"My dad wasn't there; he was on a trip," Waleed recalls. "It was me, my mom, and my brothers. We ran in to get some of our food out, and to save some of our cattle."

The incident, horrible as it was, did not scare them into leaving. They rebuilt their house, and neighbours from a nearby village helped Waleed and others from Azerné. In 2000, Janjaweed attacked Azerné again and managed to raze it completely. Still Waleed did not escape. Two years later, there was a third attack, this time on a public market in Kanaré. Waleed says the Janjaweed killed eleven people, including two women in his clan. At last he and the rest of the family escaped.

* * *

The stories blur and bend and fold into each other: always villagers living peacefully in their homeland in Darfur; for many, the first signs of real trouble in mid-to-late 2003 and the arrival of the Janjaweed. Families are displaced; many loved ones killed or left behind as survivors flee west to Chad in desperation.

Dozens of interviews later, I accompany the delegation to a Grade 8 classroom in Farchana's refugee school. Huddled together, rows upon rows of children rise and greet us in earnest song before returning to their math lesson. The blackboard hanging before them is covered in orange and white equations. Powdery chalk residue of the same two tones cakes over the fingers of their teacher.

Every time he asks them a question, a majority of students raise hands to answer, clicking their fingers, many repeatedly shouting "*ana*" ("me") for attention.

When I inquire, a member of the delegation assures me this is always their attitude: they're not putting on a show for the visit.

Class ends.

Farchana village, near the eponymous refugee camp. According to an official from a school in the camp, absenteeism is a problem because young female students are often forced into premature marriages, then into working in the village to help make ends meet.

The teacher explains the classroom may look packed, but absenteeism is a serious problem at the school. These children, though, do not play hooky to stay at home or go hang out at a shopping mall with their friends. There is probably not a shopping mall for hundreds of kilometres anyway.

"There are students who are forbidden from coming to class," the teacher says through my translator. "It's frequently the problem for girls who are pushed into premature marriages," he adds. They are instead forced to go to work at nearby Farchana village, in order to meet the needs of their families.

A boy rises from the back of the group and approaches me, carefully brushing past his peers watching seated on two colourful rugs on the ground, girls huddled on the left side of the room, boys on the right.

"He has a message for you," one of the delegates says helpfully, probably reading the bemusement on my face.

"I'm listening," I nod, and she translates.

Ever-smiling, the boy launches into an explanation of the woes students in this refugee camp will one day face: if they do graduate from the school, they are from families so poor most of them will never be able to afford higher education.

"All you can do is nod, say you understand and support their question," the supportive delegate says. No doubt she has seen her fair share of foreigners experience crushing powerlessness and guilt upon hearing this plight.

"I understand and support your question," I tell the boy.

He beams; we exchange pens as a symbol of friendship.

As we exit, Marcel reminds me people in charge of security can have a sense of humour, too. "Your pen is empty," he chuckles.

As we walk to the next station in our stop, Marcel's attention is caught by the sight of a DIS convoy holding a boy.

He walks over to them, strikes up a conversation, and returns to us.

"What happened over there?" I ask.

Raad explains the youth had tried to run away from his mother, reach the Sudanese border: a seventy-kilometre hike through totally inhospitable desert.

"What did he think he was going to be able to do?"

Raad tells me friends saw him taking a chicken from a coop for sustenance. The mother, having caught wind of his plan in the nick of time, warned the DIS, who grabbed him just before he left Farchana.

"What did he intend to do, once he reached Sudan?" I ask. The boy looks no older than ten.

I watch the DIS lecture him and send him home, with a bottle of water, after getting his promise not to try and escape again.

"Now he knows he'll get a bottle of water next time he tries that." Raad the comedian strikes again.

*   *   *

The rest of the day is spent checking in on a practical skills workshop for older refugees, and a tour of their hospital, which includes a birthing centre consisting of a couple of bare-bones rooms, one for mothers-to-be to give birth in, and the next to rest in once the work is done.

When the delegation asks me how I'd like to spend tomorrow, my last full day at Farchana, my interest returns to the boy who tried to run away to Sudan and his mother, and the tales of resource scarcity fueling conflict between displaced Darfuris and the local population.

We agree we'll do our best to work on these issues and head out of the camp.

* * *

As far as I can tell, there is only one television set in the entire U.N. compound, in the same container that holds the kitchen and a lounge.

For the second evening in a row, I sit down with Marcel and two other workers for dinner, and for the second evening in a row, the women pick programming: a terrible soap opera called *Traffic* over Marcel's preference of soccer (or, as the planet beyond North America calls it, football).

The women sit on a bigger couch across from the TV and laugh at the spectacularly cheesy drama as Marcel sulks in the corner on a single seat, mock-angry. On screen, gangsters in cheap suits make to beat up on their wives and girlfriends to a trashy stock soundtrack plucked from some Hollywood cutting-room floor. The artifice is obvious. One moment there's a wide-angle shot showing a woman on the ground and a man next to her; the next we see a close-up of the man, clearly kicking away at thin air.

Marcel sighs; the women laugh. "I need to watch something stupid like this," confesses one of them.

* * *

The morning following begins with us meeting Zafeera Babiker. In a yellow veil, matching skirt, and blue shirt, the refugee takes me and my interpreter through the walls of her tiny home. She grabs a rolled-up rug, opens it, flattens it against the sandy ground, and sits down, barefoot. Following her cue, my interpreter and I remove our footwear before doing the same.

In a small enclosure behind us, Babiker's snow-white donkey stands, leashed near a bale of hay. It hides from the sun in the shade of a brick wall barely taller than the tips of its pointy ears. I'm concerned that its incessant braying may ruin the voice recording, but it stays quiet throughout the interview.

Babiker is a single mother of five. Where in the house her children all fit is unclear to me. She keeps them fed essentially through shrewd bargaining and a lot of hard work every day. She's a part of the target refugee population the UNHCR would like to wean off dependence on firewood, a rapidly diminishing resource in the region. The UNHCR, with the help of another humanitarian organization, CORD (Christian Outreach Relief and Development), has been trying to convince people to use solar cookers instead, essentially cardboard and aluminum constructions that require daylight.

"My five children need breakfast every morning before going to school," Babiker argues. "I can't wait for sunrise to cook their food."

Thus, she relies on a more old-fashioned resource: wood, and the hole in the earth she calls her oven.

She's also hardly alone. Camp authorities have managed to give out 2,250 solar cookers to families so far, but that's a fraction of the total refugee population, and the UNHCR is fully aware that the larger the household, the less efficient the cooker. Bigger families are left off the list.

Babiker has gotten into trouble for seeking out more firewood. With what she calls an insufficient monthly allotment from authorities, she has ventured kilometres away from the camp to cut down some of her own.

Zafeera Babiker's "oven" that she uses to cook food for her five children at the Farchana refugee camp.

In this, too, she's not alone. Since arriving at the camps, I've noticed refugees who appear to be returning from long treks on foot, their donkeys loaded with stacks of broken branches.

Babiker, though, doesn't do it anymore. Not after she says nine local Chadians once stopped her, brandished knives, and hacked away at the ropes she'd planned on using to bind her precious wood. "They cut it to pieces, which they didn't return to me," she huffs. "They told me not to come back."

Babiker now buys her wood from a local merchant, or trades some of the canned goods she receives as part of her rations with other refugees. The subject is clearly a bit of a taboo. Babiker cannot name the merchant she buys her wood from, stating she does not have the information. Others at the camp tell us he's called Ahmed Abdurrahman, and is a Sudanese refugee himself, operating a sales booth at Farchana village. However, we find it empty after a trip there in a UNHCR convoy. We return to the refugee camp to find Abdurrahman resting in his home. Perspiring from the days' heat, he sits on a long, flat chair, the paunch of his stomach hidden in the folds of a white robe.

"I only sell medicine for people and cattle," he nervously says through his grey beard, denying he's ever had anything to do with selling firewood. "I never sold wood. What people say about me isn't true."

The merchant goes on to show me a barely visible scar sketched on the web space between his right thumb and fore-finger — his reward, he says, for grabbing the blade of a knife brandished at him by one of nine men who bullied him out of collecting hay for his donkey.

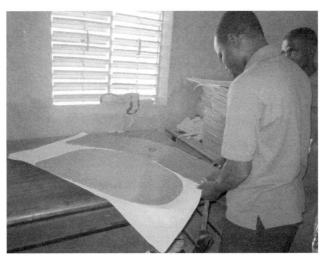

A staff worker with CORD makes a solar cooker. They're meant to wean refugees at the Farchana refugee camp off of their dependence on firewood.

*   *   *

In a quiet meeting room, my translator and I meet Muna Suliman and her son, yesterday's would-be runaway, Sami Elhaj. Seated in dusty, red-and-blue plastic chairs, neither seems particularly ecstatic to be speaking to us, and the boy spends much of the time casting his eyes downward.

Suliman says her concern is not just the risks Elhaj would run crossing the border, but what would occur once he did: namely, getting lured into the Janjaweed, the very people the family fled Darfur to escape years ago. She says she has heard of youths tricked into combat with the promise of fifty thousand to a hundred thousand Central African francs, the equivalent of C$108 to C$216. Granted, that sum goes further than it does back in Montreal, but as a suitably high price for throwing your life away, I'm not sure it qualifies.

UNHCR officials at the camp could not put a figure on the number of Darfuri refugees who try to flee back home, but tell me it's a less frequent phenomenon than it used to be.

What's clear, though, they say, is that Suliman's worries about the Janjaweed are not unfounded. They have, indeed, been known to hire young escapees who return to Sudan. My interpreter and I turn our attention to the boy. "My mom can't afford to buy me soccer cleats," he whispers miserably, his eyes on his toes poking through sandals, when I ask him why he wanted to run off and earn himself a living in Sudan.

At first I assume his posture is linked to his shame at what he's done, at having to answer our questions, but later I would read that not staring an interlocutor in the eye is a sign of respect in some non-Western cultures.

"Aren't you worried about soldiers trying to hire you away?"

The Farchana refugee camp, from which Sami Elhaj tried to run away.

I ask, but it is clearly translated into something longer, or at the very least, more intense. From the beginning of this particular session, my interpreter has appeared a little less calm than usual. His tall, lanky frame occupies the entire room, bent over the boy with almost patriarchal scrutiny. To his stern questions Elhaj answers with brief, plaintive murmurs.

"He says he wouldn't have joined," my translator turns and informs me.

Out of professional respect, I dare not ask him if he changed some of the tenor of my questions on the spot. The subject would never come up between us. Ours was beyond a simple employer/ employee relationship. Sure, he'd be getting paid for the work, but he looked also at least a decade my elder, and had an ease with navigating Chad's complicated transportation and refugee camp bureaucracy that made him more guide than interpreter.

We leave them be, a mother so frightened that the terrible past she fled would consume her family, a son so young he could not understand what that means.

* * *

My last morning in Farchana leaves me no time to speak to the refugees, as I instead calculate frantically to ensure I reach N'Djamena for an early flight out of Chad the next day.

The chaos begins when I find that a flight to Abbéché, where I'm supposed to get to N'Djamena from, has been cancelled. This means I'll never make it for the first flight out to N'Djamena, but Abbéché does have a second flight. We could probably get on that one, but there are no other Farchana–Abbéché planes.

Marcel works the phones and his clout as head of security, convinces a DIS detachment to drive me and my translator from Farchana to Abbéché, estimating that should give us just enough time to catch our flight to N'Djamena.

I recall his briefing: listening to whatever demands are thrown our way if bandits waylay us was key. Most of the time, he said, nobody's interested in harming you. They just want to rob you blind.

The trip to Abbéché passes without incident, but the layover threatens to last beyond what my schedule can afford.

The UNHCR's flight records do not include us on the schedule for the afternoon's departure to N'Djamena. And whereas Marcel had told us getting on the list would be a simple matter of explaining we were supposed to fly in the morning, the clerk we have to convince proves not to be so amenable. "Who works like this?" he protests, hovering over paperwork, demanding to know why we figured everything would be so easy.

That our instructions all stem from his own colleagues at the UNHCR does little to appease him.

Fortunes do not improve until another worker shows up. "Don't worry, Raffy," he says, with enough mischief in his tone I expect a cartoon mascot-like wink as a fuller hint that he has no problem skirting bureaucracy. "Everything will be fine."

And, sure enough, everything is. We are flown back to N'Djamena with no great trouble. My translator and I leave each other at the airport, across from the huddled taxi drivers waiting for their fares. He has made these kinds of trips several times, and I suspect there will be more in his future. I would presume he is less affected by the stories of grief we've been collecting from interviewees for the last couple of days, but I never really ask, and he doesn't bring it up, either. Strangely, instead of a common moment of reflection, our last interaction is purely transactional. I pay him his translator's wages, we wish each other good luck, and I drag my wheeled luggage over the dirt path to the cabs, taking a last look back at his tall, lanky frame walking away into the sunset. Briefly I ask myself how he'll get to his place, but I'm long past being worried. If he so easily found places to sleep outside the U.N. compounds in the bush, getting home won't be a challenge.

*   *   *

My last night in the Chadian capital is spent once more at the Bei Fang, through a reservation I'd made just as I'd arrived, prior to discovering the cheaper accommodations elsewhere. There is another early-morning wake-up call the next day to catch a flight.

Authorities are a little more serious about carrying out their jobs than they were during my first few treks to Hassan

Djammous. Maybe they do not enjoy trifling with international departures. "You don't have the stamp," one immigration official leafing through my passport says, as I approach the metal detector and conveyor belt for my carry-on.

I do not quite understand. "All I have are stamps," I want to protest and point out his taste is rather elitist if not a single one among the million I've been forced to acquire since my arrival meets his standards. I bite my tongue, and he explains a colleague standing behind a glass booth to the side must fill out an exit form and then stamp my travel document.

The officer in question grabs my passport and begins his work when I walk over. I interpret the look on his face as one of bewilderment at the length and complicated nature of my name. He makes me spell it out, which I've got down to a science after years of dealing with public-relations specialists over the phone at my day job.

"Address?" he then asks, and I slowly begin to tell him how to write that, too.

"You know I could probably fill it out; it'd be faster," I offer, but his brisk "No" implies he's insulted at the very idea.

"There, it's over," he says, after asking a few more questions, scratching his pen and adding the million-and-first stamp. But instead of handing me my documentation, he presses his hand against it on the table and grins.

"So I can be on my way?" I ask, gesturing toward the hostage paperwork and pretending not to understand what's going on.

"A little something so I can buy myself a Coke," he affirms rather than asks.

I hand him the pocket change that remains of my Central African francs, pick up what's mine, and walk over to the metal detector and customs area.

The guard there is visibly irritated. I may have given his friend too much and left him nothing. "What's this?" he asks suspiciously, about a tiny, black and silver head-mount flashlight in my carry-on luggage.

I tell him its functions, hoping my manner is courteous but firm enough to clarify I will not be parting with it, while I fully await a second take on the smartphone and restaurant incident.

"That's very neat," his colleague says softly.

"Yes, it can be very helpful," I tell her.

They drop the subject. "Well, are you going to return to Chad?" she asks, with exaggerated enthusiasm. I do not know what to say, and so choose to commit nothing at all.

The Ethiopian Airlines plane has a warm meal but no in-flight entertainment, the opposite of what was advertised on my e ticket, but no complaints from my grumbling stomach.

Again my knowledge of English earns me a seat next to the emergency exit, where I take a quick look at instructions, which also appear in Amharic, one of Ethiopia's official languages.

I become excited at the sight of some of the characters, which are identical to ones that appear in my mother language, Armenian. They are scrawled in red next to their English-language counterparts, on a white sticker covering the door handle and another above the door panel, explaining it is for emergency use only. I snap a couple of pictures and my finger hovers hesitatingly over the send button on my phone, as I ponder the ridiculous overseas messaging costs. Then I text the images to my siblings regardless, my wireless carrier's greed be darned.

One last connection between my ancestral homeland and the place where I first met genocide survivors.

Chapter 4

The Country That Would Rebuild

The Kigali Genocide Memorial Centre sits, prim and pristine, in a garden surveying Rwanda's leafy green capital.

Flames flicker in a black bowl resting on a white pedestal, itself installed in a small pool on the red brick walkway leading to the building. I recollect another memorial fire, blazing thousands of kilometres away at the Dzidzernagapert ("swallow's fortress," in Armenian) genocide monument and museum in Armenia, on the outskirts of Yerevan.

There, the eternal flame juts out of a mechanism encircled by twelve grey slabs bowing toward one another, each representing one of twelve Armenian-populated provinces lost in eastern Turkey. A wall running the length of its manicured lawn bears the names of the same provinces, each carved out in Armenian letters. A stele, also grey, rises next to the construction, symbolizing the rebirth of the Armenian people. In a nearby garden, trees planted by visiting delegations from other countries cast their shadows, their origins marked on plaques at the base of their trunks.

In Kigali, bouquets of flowers, wrapped in transparent packaging and neat purple ribbons, also rest on the grounds of the centre. It's all in remembrance of the nearly one million people who lost their lives in the small African state in 1994.

The Rwandan genocide was the result of long-simmering tensions between the country's ruling Hutu majority, and its Tutsi minority. Colonial Belgium had played the two sides against each other for decades, leaving them at each other's throats following Rwanda's independence in 1962. The Hutus grabbed power, but the struggle didn't end there. A guerrilla Tutsi movement squared off against the regime. By the early '90s, Hutu president Juvénal Habyarimana began to speak of peace accords with the Tutsis' Rwanda Patriotic Front (RPF), much to the chagrin of extremists in his ranks. On April 6, 1994, Habyarimana's plane was shot out of the sky. It's still unclear who pulled the trigger: Hutu hardliners, unhappy with his compromises, have been blamed, and so have the Tutsis. What is clear is the event signalled the beginning of the end for peace. For a hundred days, the Interahamwe Hutu militia slaughtered Tutsis and moderate Hutus indiscriminately, until the Tutsi RPF managed to turn the tide and end the massacres.

Inside the museum, sensitive visitors may find themselves fast reduced to tears. Down its somber, moodily lit corridors, panels and displays outlining the dark history are often accompanied by pictures of victims, examples of the weapons used to take their lives away, or pieces of clothing of all different sizes. The smaller shoes and garments leave no doubt as to the killers' success in wiping out just about everyone, regardless of age. Here, it's explained, two young sisters, whose favourite toy was a doll they shared, died when a hand grenade landed in their bathtub. There, a brother and sister are said to have been attacked by Interahamwe and killed by machete on a visit to their grandmother's house. My heart skips a beat as I picture either scenario, involving my nephew instead of these strangers.

One showcase stops me in my tracks: a child's blue, tattered blanket, stamped with the name and likeness of Superman. Talk about a symbol of Western impotence. In 1994, much of the West stood and watched, offering slightly offended comments as Rwandans were slaughtered. The United States roused itself to raising concerns about "acts of genocide." The scarcity of any kind of humanitarian engagement was astonishing. Reporting on that, one Reuters journalist, in an exchange that's become notorious in literature about media from the era, exposed the extreme nature of the government's double-speak by asking a spokesperson, "How many acts of genocide does it take to make a genocide?"

Superman, that ultimate avatar of Truth, Justice, and The American Way (a likeness of whose colourful costume I used to sport as pajamas in my early childhood, and whose alter ego may have found himself pitching such a hardball question in his day job as a reporter), was busy dealing with returning to life after his much-hyped death in comic books the previous year at the hands of some mindless interstellar pugilist. Of course, the problem with spinning sci-fi tales about invincible champions of morality is you can't have atrocities such as the Rwandan genocide exist in the same universe as they do, because how could Kal-El simply look on while so many people died? You wouldn't just be scratching against the boundaries of the form, you'd be clawing right through them. I shudder to calculate how much mainstream media coverage Clark Kent's temporary doodled demise earned in comparison to the very real and permanent deaths of hundreds of thousands of Rwandans.

A roomful of panels at the centre also looks back on other contemporary crimes against humanity, from the Jewish Holocaust to the Cambodian and Armenian genocides. Outside the museum, Kigali is still a shock to the senses. The temperature hovers around a soothing twenty degrees Celsius mark, a far cry from Chad's barely bearable forties. There, plastic bags dotted the desert landscape and clung to dried branches, rippling in the wind. Here, they're banned anywhere outside the Kigali International Airport, where, upon landing, I watched security guards insist another traveller toss the shrink-wrap around their luggage into a trash bin before leaving the premises.

The sidewalks of Kigali's tree-lined streets are constantly swept clean by public workers, and there's no shortage of tourists, many passing through on a whirlwind tour of several African countries.

Rwandans are graceful and cheerful hosts to outsiders. In Internet cafés, workers will sometimes remind you about the sporadic power outages, encouraging you to be careful when you use their Wi-Fi connections.

After some frustration trying to hook up my smartphone to local carriers, I walk into a small electronics store to buy a cheap, temporary flip-top. The salesman is appalled at what he sees as a waste of money, and spends several minutes trying to figure out a connection on my current device before giving up. He makes no attempt to sell me a high-end phone, and actually takes the time to accompany me to another nearby shop that sells prepaid minutes, since it's not a practice at his store. The bright red, branded polo shirt wrapped around his thin frame and the similarly coloured baseball cap covering his thinning head of hair must immediately mark him as somebody working for the competition when we enter this second business, but nobody blinks as he guides me through my options there, giddily smiling the whole time.

Imagine this in North America.

It's tough to reconcile this reality with the fact Rwanda's essentially a post-apocalyptic society.

My hostel is a very symbol of that. The Discover Rwanda is hidden from the main hustle and bustle of Kigali on a quiet downhill street, behind white gates emblazoned with its logo, depicting a yellow palm tree and hunched gorilla in silhouette on a triangular green background. It is funded by the Aegis Trust, the same British organization that oversees the memorial centre and finances genocide-related reconciliation workshops. Its clientele includes an ever-shifting influx of European adventurers, who cheerfully spend late nights mingling on the large veranda with its view of nearby woods. Of course, on days when it won't stop raining, the mingling is rather a necessity, with the covered deck about as far as some choose to venture.

On my second evening in the country, I set up a meeting at the hostel with Elvis Nibomari, a bright journalism graduate who is to be my translator as needed during the stay. When a colleague of mine linked us through Facebook, Elvis in his profile pic sported a large 'fro haircut. The clean-cut young man who shows up instead, done up in a freshly pressed white dress shirt, recognizes me much faster than I him.

"I'll just have a Coke," Elvis insists, when I ask if I may get him a beer from the bar. We chat quietly in the hostel lobby, sipping our drinks as we figure out a fair wage for him on days where I will require his help. Many of the people I am to meet in Rwanda do speak English or French, meaning I won't need to have Elvis at my side as often as I relied on my translator in Chad.

*   *   *

Occasionally, despite its external insouciance, Kigali reminds you how dangerous a place it was barely two decades ago. Unlike in N'Djamena, just about everyone feels free to walk about the city day and night — but enter as innocuous a place as a shopping mall and you may have to agree to a metal-detector test.

And you only need to dig a little deeper to see Rwanda's still very much figuring out how to come together again. Genocide perpetrators — and their victims — sometimes are literal neighbours. Their children attend reconciliation workshops together, listening to tales of how the massacres unfolded, and how they must let those wounds heal.

Simultaneously, federal attorneys rack up long hours at work tracking down escaped *génocidaires*, in the belief the country will never truly rise above its still-fresh past horrors unless those criminals are brought to justice.

In fact, my arrival in Kigali closely follows that of another man who has also recently made the trip over from Canada. But Léon Mugesera packed his bags much more reluctantly. The "spokesman of hatred," as media have grown to call him, escaped Rwanda in 1992, two years before the massacres began, after allegedly publicly inciting them. Mugesera then spent nearly two decades as a university professor in Quebec City.

But at last he lost judicial arguments against Rwanda's demanding his return home, there to stand in court against charges of inciting hatred.

And one of the first people I am to meet in Kigali leads the pack of attorneys searching for those like Mugesera.

Chapter 5

He Who Chases Genocide

The space between justice and revenge thins or thickens for genocide survivors; sometimes, it feels, according to the ebb and flow of time.

In 1921, a scant few years after the Armenian genocide, Talaat Pasha, Ottoman minister of the interior and one of the triumvirate of Young Turk leaders who planned and executed it, was tracked down and shot in Berlin by Soghomon Tehlirian. Not quite twenty-five when he pulled the trigger, Tehlirian had lost his mother, his father, sisters, and brothers to the deportations leading up to the genocide in 1915. Reportedly, Tehlirian repeatedly shot Talaat in the head, to make sure he would not escape alive. Not surprisingly, Armenians have immortalized Talaat's assassination in a catchy song, with a chorus that suggests it is a tale best told around glasses of wine.

The person modern Armenians consider their Adolf Hitler had been hiding out in Germany, after being tried in absentia at the Allied Forces–run Turkish courts martial in 1919–1920, and found guilty. Shortly after he did his deed, Tehlirian was tried in a Berlin court. During the judicial proceedings, he told the courtroom how he had seen his mother's corpse in a dream, chastising him for not having killed Talaat yet. "You are no longer my son," he recalled the cadaver's rebuke.

Tehlirian was found not guilty and released.

I vaguely recall my jealousy during casting in a theatrical adaptation of Tehlirian's trial in grade school. A friend of mine netted the star role, and the teacher directing the project explained "You look like a judge," placing me behind a desk with a gavel in my hand. That a copy of the play's minimalist script was available for my discreet perusal on the desk, masquerading as a pile of "court documents," was small compensation.

Tehlirian's action is seen by most Armenians as being inspired by a desire for justice; others, however, deem it as being motivated simply by a wish for vengeance. Such a view is given some validity in that a not-uncommon first name for Armenian men is "Vrej," which can also be modified to fit women with "Vrejouhi." It translates into English as "vengeance." Imagine the awkward looks a person with such a moniker might receive if they were asked to explain its meaning. By comparison, "Raffy," which means something like "rising light," or "lightning that goes up," usually gets a confused "that's … kind of cool, I guess."

Few, if any, official sentences were carried out for those found guilty in the murky courts-martial affair. And if you have any doubts as to official Turkey's opinion on the validity of these verdicts, look no further than the tomb of Talaat Pasha, who, repatriated to his homeland by none other than the Nazi regime in 1943, lies buried in Istanbul on the Hill of Eternal Liberty, so named with no hint of irony.

Armenians have not had much of a kick at traditional justice mechanisms. Like Talaat, other direct conspirers in the crime were gunned down, instead. And now Armenians cheer

Jean Bosco Siboyintore is the head of the genocide fugitives tracking unit in Kigali, Rwanda.

any time another country joins the community of nations that have recognized the genocide as such.

There has been an easier path for Jews seeking justice after the Holocaust; though, there, too, it is unclear whether every war criminal has been brought to stand trial. Simon Wiesenthal, one Holocaust survivor, famously dedicated his life to catching Nazis, going so far as to track them down in corners of the world such as Buenos Aires, Argentina. This narrative has inspired a lot of stories over the years.

In fact, that space between justice and revenge, thinning and thickening, has inspired some of my favourite fiction: works such as Canadian-Armenian director Atom Egoyan's *Ararat*, and Quentin Tarantino's pulpy *Inglourious Basterds*, which basically spins a Second World War revenge fantasy out of the Holocaust.

Like the Rwandan story, the story of the Armenian genocide is not very familiar to the world. In Canada, Roméo Dallaire's *Shake Hands with the Devil*, a memoir of his time as a U.N. peacekeeper in Rwanda, did do much to raise public awareness of the terrible events in that country. However, neither instance of genocide has penetrated popular consciousness to the point of inspiring many works of fiction. But, as in the case of the Jews, the Rwandans do have some chance of meting out justice, as hard as it sometimes is to find missing *génocidaires*.

Some people in Rwanda now have taken on roles similar to Wiesenthal's. There is a man who plays dad to Rwanda's traumatized genocide survivors and coaxes them into identifying their assailants, but he is tough to find. Jean Bosco Siboyintore and his genocide fugitives tracking unit are in no fancy government building at the centre of Kigali.

Instead, I am provided nebulous directions to have myself dropped off near a shopping mall on the outskirts of the city. Then I must walk into a well-treed suburban neighbourhood.

The unit's offices are tucked away in a discreet, brown-bricked bungalow. The point, Siboyintore tells me when we're face to face across his wooden, paperwork- and binder-covered desk at last, is to relax genocide survivors as much as possible when they arrive to tell their tales.

Siboyintore is rigid and professional, a fastidious dresser in a full, navy-blue suit, with a white-and-blue-striped shirt, and gold tie. He looks such a lawyer's lawyer I am almost sure he sleeps in his business attire, ready at a mobile phone's vibration, beep, or blinking light to pounce on a new prosecution.

"They keep running, they keep running," he says, of the 1,092 genocide fugitives his unit knows about. Of them, it has located 134 in twenty-three countries in Africa, Europe, and North and South America.

Siboyintore tells me the unit has issued indictments or arrest warrants for each of those 134. For him, it's essential work. He says reconciliation cannot really be achieved without justice.

I consider the scope of the enterprise as we speak: more than eight hundred thousand Rwandan Tutsis and moderate Hutus dead, in the blink of an eye, relatively speaking; nearly twenty years later, many of those responsible still on the loose; judicial work that goes on longer for those who are caught.

The math is daunting. Siboyintore, though, is optimistic. "They can run but they will not hide for long," he says.

The soft-spoken Léon Mugesera, for example, is at last back home, his pretrial proceedings to begin in a few days.

Siboyintore assures me many of the people on his unit's list are alleged high-level brains behind the genocide: planners who not only carried out the killings but directed underlings.

The pale yellow walls of the unit's HQ feature posters showing them off: black-and-white thumbnail photos of unsmiling men; big, red letters asking anyone who has seen them to spill the information.

Siboyintore's days begin early, at 7:00 a.m., as he plots how to catch the fugitives. He is supposed to leave work around 5:00 p.m., he says, at last offering the barest hint of humour, but he frequently overshoots that goal. "I can even come home and go back to my office whenever there is a need," he says.

That, perhaps, is what it takes to fight the odds of so many escapees, but can the overtime labour of a handful of prosecutors begin to act as a counterbalance? What motivates a man like Siboyintore? Where does he fit on the sliding scale from justice to vengeance? I come at the question again and again throughout our interview.

"I have seen genocide," he offers, though saying nothing else that suggests he seeks revenge. He launches into dramatic, declarative sentences about justice and society, with the sort of pregnant pauses he must make at the drop of a hat in courtrooms.

Behind him, white cardboard banners with scribbled job descriptions in black, green, and red occupy several of the walls. "Core skills of conducting an interview," one reads. Clearly, this man is a pro, and he knows exactly how I'm trying to steer him into opening up.

Instead, with admittedly little resistance by yours truly, he pushes the conversation toward Rwanda's difficulties securing the international community's full co-operation in tracking down war criminals. Only in 2011 did the U.N. give its okay for one of its own war crimes defendants to be transferred to Rwanda — four years after the country's parliament abolished capital punishment. The world turned its back here during Armageddon, and now it barely trusts the survivors to sort out law and order. "You can understand the situation," Siboyintore says, diplomatically enough, alluding to the death penalty concern.

But emotion seeps in soon, with his mentions of the U.N.'s old fears that the Rwandan judiciary is not independent from its government. The latter is, after all, led by Tutsi president Paul Kagame, the same man who fought both the Hutu regime prior to the genocide and the Interahamwe during the massacres as the head of the Rwanda Patriotic Front.

"How do you measure independence of judiciary?" Siboyintore asks. If it's by the number and type of obtained verdicts, he says, the international community's response makes little sense. "[Rwandan judges] have acquitted hundreds of cases, they have convicted hundreds of cases," he says, suggesting the former would have been impossible without judicial independence.

At any rate, now at least, Siboyintore is happy. Mugesera is one of the most important fugitives his team has wanted to bring in. The "spokesman of hatred" has made noise about how fair his trial could be in Kigali. He insisted, for example, that all proceedings unfold in French, only for the court to refuse his request. "He knows Kinyarwanda, a language he has been speaking since he was born," Siboyintore shrugs, saying the man was just looking to put on a show.

I endeavour, again, to have him speak about what he lived through in 1994, but we remain in the realm of generalities. "What did I see in genocide?" he repeats the question I have asked, "the killings, genocide itself, killings that were committed in broad day."

Rwandans have moved on further from their atrocity than the Darfuris I met exiled in Chad. Speaking of the past too specifically releases forgotten memories. In Chad, where refugees make ends meet in the desert through the inadequately budgeted kindness of the international community, talk is therapy. Here, where Rwandans go to work and interact with their families and friends in a society that has painstakingly normalized itself, talk is trauma.

I try one last time. After all, he knows my story. I'd already given him The Lecture, told him of my personal interest in genocide: my great-grandfather's imprisonment and death in the land of my ancestors, my seven-year-old grandfather's goodbye to his dad, how he and the rest of the family escaped to Lebanon....

This was a process I had used in Chad, too. You could call it a tragedy trade: telling survivors my own family history in exchange for theirs.

But with Siboyintore it has yielded nothing. He avoids personal details more than ever the third time around, choosing to rattle off bullet points from his CV. "I have prosecuted hundreds of cases of genocide," he says, explaining his experience in the milieu goes back to 1996.

Siboyintore is a collector of stories, not a storyteller. No doubt opening up too much about justice versus revenge could hurt a well-cultivated professional neutrality.

I leave him to his work, as he amicably offers to let me know the exact date and time of Mugesera's first court appearance.

Chapter 6

Lost Tourist in the Mist

Out of breath, I remove my sneakers, once a combination of squeaky-clean white, grey, and shiny embossed-sports-logo green, now all of that lost in a uniform layer of mud. I teeter onto the deck of my Kigali hostel, worried about sullying the clean wooden floor with dirt. The hems of my pants are also lined in it, but at least I have an extra pair of those.

The runners, I've already decided on my way back from an excursion into Rwanda's mountainous depths, are finished. Exhausted, cramped, and weighed down by my backpack, I'm thankful to be alive myself, at all.

A staffer looks at me with bewilderment, then breaks into a knowing grin. "Ah, Kinigi," she says.

No doubt I'm not the first foolish foreigner she has witnessed who's tried going to see gorillas during wet season in the rainforest with completely inappropriate footwear.

* * *

The Discover Rwanda Youth Hostel's clientele is so intimate you gradually start to recognize most people staying there, especially when the same faces greet you at the roomy café across the street, where everyone gathers mostly for the slightly faster Wi-Fi service.

On a particularly busy day at said establishment, I find myself searching for a place to sit. A German guest of Discover spots me, his rough-and-tumble demeanor clearly more of an explorer's than my own. For one thing, it is a large, traveller's backpack he removes off a nearby couch to make space, not a student's. His face is covered in the kind of stubble that suggests he doesn't have to work for days to come, his hair with a fisherman's hat, and the single, sharp tooth of some wild animal hangs on a pendant around his neck. We don't say much besides hello, as he carries on with an apparently hilarious video call conversation in his native language, ear buds stuck in his ears.

Later on, René Wollenschein introduces himself and says he — like most European travellers I will meet in Rwanda — is on a quick tour through a handful of different African countries.

Rwanda's on his list particularly for the gorilla sightseeing opportunities. "Want to go?" René asks, saying he intends to buy a US$500 ticket — valid for exactly one day.

After weeks of speaking to genocide survivors, it's, frankly, tempting, especially as I've been listening to all the other excursions people with more free time on their hands — such as René — will be able to undertake. Besides, the idea of this trek has been somewhere in the back of my mind ever since I'd decided Rwanda would be one of my destinations, though with some reservations.

"Who are you going to interview on the weekend anyway?" he asks skeptically, when I object about survivors I've been struggling to line up for meetings. Nobody's called me back yet.

I concede the point but bring up the price issue. After all, the same amount of money would go a long way in case of unforeseen emergencies, and I still had about twenty-one days of travelling to manage.

"When's the next time you'll be in Rwanda?" he asks. Another good point. There's also that, in the unlikely event I do return anytime soon, I would have to pay more. Rwanda's about to raise its ape ticket prices to US$750 in a couple of weeks.

I tell René I'll think about it, and leave it at that.

A few hours later, having only booked interviews for the next week, and verified René did buy his ticket by texting him on my old-school, temporary, "stupid" phone, I chance it and purchase my own.

There's still a little bit of dread in my gut. A journalist friend of mine who spent time in Rwanda warned me not to make the gorilla trip until my last few days there, so my body would have had time to adjust to the country's mountain climate.

Not only am I neglecting her advice, my disobedience follows a session of altitude sickness. The strange condition, mostly a shortness of breath, has been with me throughout my first few days in Kigali. Any laborious physical exercise brings it on. I've attempted to fight it with generous amounts of tea and pain-relief pills. I'm perplexed: altitude sickness has never bothered me on previous trips to mountainous countries.

I make my sickness more difficult by packing along my clunker of a laptop, along with cameras and audio recorders, being paranoid about leaving any of that stuff with the rest of my luggage. Essentially, it's just most of my travel wardrobe that stays behind in Kigali, locked in my room. So I'm not in tip-top physical shape, and with nearly fifteen kilograms on my back, when I set out on the adventure.

Travelling from Kigali to Kinigi is easy enough: a few hours on an inexpensive bus packed really tight. The only annoyance is a seatmate who starts to inquire about Quebec, and whether or not I can help him immigrate. His overly adventurous hands go as far as reaching for my backpack ("You need some help with that," he suggests), making me question my choice of loading it with all my electronic equipment. "I'll be fine," I say, rather firmly.

In Kinigi, there's a brief wait at a bus station to switch vehicles. I busy myself taking pictures of the darkening sky and a looming peak of the Volcanoes National Park, blanketed in greenery. Overstuffed knapsack hanging on my back, I could only look like more of a tourist if I also had my face buried in a comically large map, too. I notice a group of local teenagers begins pointing and laughing.

"Give me all your money," one of them quips. I smile and walk away.

I catch up with René once I hop off the second bus, at a hotel he's found near the foot of the mountain range, Kinigi Guest House.

Here's where it can get complicated: the trip can cost you way more money. The gorilla tours start quite early on the next morning, but from a prohibitive distance away. Chauffeurs offer their services for a good $80 to $100. They know you've already spent hundreds, and are unlikely to refuse at this point.

René and I are lucky, though. In the guest house's dining area, a sprawling wooden courtyard that looks way fancier than the shack where I'll be spending the night, we befriend an American couple who have moved to Rwanda and own an SUV. They say they will drive us to the national park the next day.

The big move hasn't been a whole lot of trouble, they explain, frustrating their two pet cats more than it has them. The felines aren't fans of the mosquito netting that surrounds the couple's bed, ensnaring themselves as they try to clamber aboard to lie down with them.

In the morning we are separated. The Americans have already seen the gorillas and are here for another sight: the golden monkeys, and René is somehow banded with another group of people who have shown up for the apes.

His last act of kindness is to reach for a stubbornly sealed bottle of water I'm struggling with and to remove its cap with an effortless twist of his fingers. He hands it back to me silently, too nice to remark on my sudden weakness. I want to explain about my lingering altitude-related queasiness and heavy bag, but feel it would come off as an excuse.

I'm teamed up with an Austrian, Marlene Johler; a Swiss, Julien Haarman; and a Scotsman, Andrew Thorburn. The latter two are old friends, and have travelled from Kigali, where they appear to be staying long-term. Johler is yet another of the many Europeans I meet on the jaunt through Africa. From the stories she and Haarman share, it's obvious this, for them, is but one of many extreme outdoor adventures.

We're packed in an SUV with two guides, and I volunteer to place myself all the way in the back, bumping and rolling up and down against some luggage as we're driven on a rocky road to the starting point of our hike. Our main guide says we'll have a good ninety minutes of trekking to do before we reach the heights where our gorilla group, the Amahoro, tend to hang out.

We all tell each other we're excited and ready as we begin to walk, but, truth be told, my simple Nikes and weighty backpack increasingly seem like terrible ideas. At least Thorburn and Haarman also have an equally lousy sense of what shoes to wear: the only one with proper hiking boots is Marlene.

That becomes clear fairly quickly on the ground. As we meander past some farms, everyone keeps up a fairly even pace, though we almost forget what we're here for in the first place when we are distracted by some adorable baby lambs that temporarily trot alongside us. However, Johler springs ahead as soon as we march into the thick rainforest.

I lag behind everyone else. Our second guide, mostly there for security, brings up the rear as well, though by design and not poor planning. "Slowly," he occasionally whispers to me, as if I'm a child learning to walk, while I trip and tumble through the muck. "Slippery," he then adds. Nimble and agile in his thigh-high rubber boots, he casually balances a rifle on his back as he strides along. Apparently, curious buffaloes sometimes wander a little too close to hikers for comfort: he is to shoot in the air and scare them off if that were to happen.

It doesn't, though. We hear the chirps of birds high above in the trees around us, and plenty of bugs buzz about, too, but those are the only immediate signs of wildlife.

Of course, my sneakers soon become so enveloped in mud I am carrying two size-eleven swamps on my feet, half-expecting a tadpole to emerge from between my shoelaces. The bubbly, squishy sound effects somehow remind me of a childhood friend's parents' kitchen ages ago, his mom cutting up a macaroni dish for us during dinner.

After a while, the backpack turns into quite a burden and it's obvious that I'm slowing everyone else down. One of the guides snatches a dead tree branch well-suited to serve as a walking stick and hands it over.

But it's Julien Haarman, I've got to say, who is most sympathetic, frequently hanging back like some sort of watchful forest spirit, asking to carry my bag for me. Though as wrong-headed in

It looks like I stepped into chocolate pudding.

his choice of shoes as I am, it's clear from his easier bearing and lighter packing he's more of an outdoorsman than I am. There is not a trace of sweat on his brow, and he shows no hint of laboured breathing. A part of me can't shake the suspicion he would have already made the hike if he were not in need of a guide, or hiking boots. Pride pushes me to politely decline his help, as every line of fatigue on my face puts the lie to my nonchalance.

We keep marching, enveloped in humidity, yet still wearing long sleeves and raingear for fear of exotic insect stings and rainfall. We all showed so much enthusiasm for the expedition nobody dares ask the perennially annoying "Are we there yet?" I presume the guides would be too polite to say "We're turning this tour around unless you quit yelling" if we did break into such a chorus.

I get an uncomfortable flashback to a failed hike in Matagalpa, Nicaragua, in 2006. With another group of randomly united travellers I had set out hoping to see howler monkeys hanging way above us in a forest and we had all wound up running away, howling ourselves as carnivorous ants nipped at our heels.

All of a sudden our main guide tells us we're close and insists we all put down our backpacks.

I voice some concern over this, citing all my equipment.

"You should be happy to be leaving your backpack behind," Thorburn says, as our guides point out the absurdity of my distress: there is nobody to rifle through my belongings for kilometres around.

"Hey, what's that gorilla doing with your backpack?" Haarman jests.

Alleviated of our carry-ons, we walk a little more briskly, though by now I'm so tired I never advance beyond last in our quartet.

"We should all stick together," Haarman says, again making sure I'm still breathing as I catch up to the rest.

Then, in the midst of some forgettable conversation, he asks me to be quiet. I'm about to object, but he points me to the reason for his request.

A couple of steps ahead of us, muscular, glistening, jet-black back turned to our faces, a member of the Amahoro munches away at vegetation, bushes and branches bristling under its considerable girth.

The creature's calm is what surprises me most. Here's a bunch of strangers loudly and clumsily stomping through its habitat, whirring away with their video recorders and making obnoxious flashes with their still cameras, but it carries on with no sign of annoyance.

Thorburn would later put it best. "It was like they could be almost in our living room and we could be sitting there

This little fellow's — ahem — monkeying around alone was worth the hike.

having a glass of tea and they'd just be playing around," he would confide.

We shake off our weariness at the excitement of meeting more Amahoro. Our guide begins to grunt like a gorilla to announce our presence, and the beasts reply. He turns to us and says we have their welcome to stay and take pictures. I record some of the exchange and tell him I'll be unable to distinguish between the audio of his own perfectly imitated simian speak and that of the animals. He laughs it off as unearned flattery for his linguistic skills.

There are only around three hundred gorillas left in Rwanda, our guide tells us. The Amahoro number eighteen, and have a reputation for being among the friendlier ones. Their very name means "peace." They demonstrate their cool attitude by calmly posing for photographs.

The silverback, the tribe's leader, sits with pride and confidence watching over us, glancing at its own giant fist once in a while. Like the rest of its kin, it mostly walks around on all fours, the hunch hiding its immense strength but a little.

"Oh, look at the baby," Marlene points out. We all stare down at the knee-high munchkin, flipping and flopping on the ground for our amusement. Our guide explains it's one year old, then starts emitting short, fast groans. The gorilla looks on wild-eyed, with rapt attention.

"He's listening to you," I say, amused. The guide tells us he's essentially making amusing baby noises. "I do that with my nephew," I add. Thorburn says the kid's parents may be none too amused at the comparison. I do not ask him which kid's parents he is talking about.

Encouraged by being in the spotlight, the baby continues its acrobatic tricks for us, rolling around in the dirt, gripping a leaf with its claw-like toes and stuffing it into its mouth.

But here, too, amidst all this wonder, I'm unable to quite leave man's inhumanity behind. "That's number two," our guide tells us, pointing to another of the bigger gorillas.

"There's something wrong with that one," he says as the primate quietly scrutinizes its visitors. Unlike the other members of the Amahoro, number two keeps a considerable distance from the group. It takes us a moment to register the stump where its left hand should be, as its wrist is almost totally covered in black fur.

"Traps," the guide offers, as the only explanation.

As one ape sits perfectly still, we decide it's a good opportunity to snap portraits of ourselves in front of it.

I capture an amazing one of Haarman, grinning ear to ear as the gorilla looks on, soft-focus, at his back.

I pass him my camera, hoping he can reproduce the effect. But no sooner does he aim the shutter at me than he, Thorburn, and Johler all start to look on with mingled expressions of fear and laughter. "Don't be afraid," Julien says, and warns me two gorillas have begun to fight behind my back.

My look in the snapshots pretty clearly reflects my opinion of two eight-hundred-pound wrestlers going at it a couple of steps away from me.

Still, I remain perfectly still ... at least until someone's finger gently double-taps my shoulder. In half-a-second, I calculate every other human for a considerable radius is in front of me.

By the time one of our guides says "That means you have to move," I've already careered out of the way with a breathless "No kidding."

All your traumas and anxieties fall away in such a moment. Forget about genocide, immigration, the weight of history, seeking refuge, or retribution. Everything becomes about survival when a creature that could crush your skull one-handed if it so chose wants you to step aside.

Behind me, the gentleman gorilla walks the path I've cleared for him, eyes betraying a sense of exasperation at having had to get its paw on a damn, dirty human in the first place.

We wrap up with the Amahoro right on cue, a fine rain settling over us shortly after the end of the session.

"We're lucky today," our guide says, adding the apes stay hidden during storms. That would be why it was so easy for me to buy a ticket with only a day's notice, since most people plan their trip during Rwanda's more sneakers-friendly dry season.

On the way back, we stop and pick up our abandoned backpacks, which look untouched. I'm too embarrassed to verify an ape hasn't indeed repossessed my laptop. Besides, the bag sure still feels the right weight. Haarman offers his assistance again.

"Maybe in another twenty minutes or so, when I'm really dead," I push back.

"Maybe we should do it before you're really dead," he says, but we all return to the base camp in one piece.

Despite being the only one with a whole lot of grey hair, Thorburn appears the least exhausted of us all. He skips lightly over the misty farmland near the forest, his long poncho casting the silhouette of a banshee adrift from its Scottish Highlands.

We reunite with René at the Kinigi Guest House, where we hear the gorillas his group tracked down, the Susa, made him earn his excellent pictures, temporarily running and dodging him and the other explorers.

* * *

Bumming a ride off of Thorburn and Haarman back to Kigali in a hired car, in exchange for a round of drinks in Kinigi, I muse about the week ahead: Léon Mugesera's court dates, several interviews with genocide survivors ... and, then, preparations for Turkey, with its reputation for disdain toward reporters — or anyone, really — who ask uncomfortable questions about the Armenian genocide.

Silver lining: at Discover Rwanda, the lovely staff insists my runners have a lot of mileage left to them, and will be good as new after they're done cleaning them up.

Chapter 7

Rosette

Among the bric-a-brac littering the wooden desk in my hostel room is a genocide survivor's business card.

Okay, that's not what is literally written next to Rosette Sebasoni's name, but it may as well be. Parts of the thirty-four-year-old insurance broker's tale are told to anyone who pays close attention at the Kigali Memorial Centre, one of the many survivor stories on display.

When Sebasoni agreed to an interview, I did not know quite how close she worked to Discover Rwanda.

We convene in front of Discover's main entrance.

The petite woman with short-cropped hair and a snappy blue business skirt and jacket ensemble who greets me is warm, bustling with energy. You'd never know she was showing up to relive her personal part in one of modern history's most terrible chapters.

We first sit down on the deck. But there's too much noise and I suggest moving to the lobby inside, countering her idea of venturing to my room. I start recording and there are again too many passersby for the sensitive microphone, what with Discover's main cash register right behind us. "I think we're going to go to your room," she says, and I do not resist further.

By my own fairly generous standards, my room is a complete mess. Currency from three different countries colours my desk. Mosquito netting is strewn haphazardly around my bed, itself covered with many sets of clothes, my laptop, the spent batteries I've hastily exchanged for fresh ones in my audio recorder, and my box of malaria pills. The only reason my open suitcase doesn't greet us with a display of its innards, too, is because the suspicious traveller in me unfailingly locks it shut every time before leaving the premises.

Rosette doesn't blink as I clumsily apologize, and offers to sit on the mattress. But I convince her to take the only chair, and scatter my belongings to make myself a spot in the chaos instead.

Remarkably, she doesn't need to hear The Lecture. Rosette believes the story of the Rwandan genocide and its victims should be known far and wide, no tragedy trade is necessary to coax the details of what happened to the Sebasonis out of her.

She was on the cusp of turning sixteen when her life turned to hell. Rosette lived with her parents, Aphrodis Sebasoni and Dorothée Kandamutsa; her older brother, Freddy Mutanguha Sebasoni; four younger sisters, Consolée, Angélique, Florence, and Illuminée; and an adopted sister, Jeanne, in the district of Kibuye. It is roughly a two-hour drive west of Kigali, near the shores of Lake Kivu. Now only Rosette and Freddy remain.

At first, a Hutu acquaintance told them they could hide at his house, saying the killings were a type of passing fad, and they would be safe once it was all over.

Slim protection, at best. "How are these Tutsis still alive?" asked Interahamwe militia who dropped by for a visit on April 14, 1994, seven days after the start of the massacres.

They took her parents right then and there. "You can't be scared," is one of the last sentences Rosette remembers her father and mother pronouncing. "We can't stay here," they also said … and then, optimistically, "You will live," before they were carted off.

An Interahamwe tried to strike a bargain with the terrified Rosette, not for Dorothée's life, but for a faster death. "Your mom told me you have a little bit of money," he told the girl. "Can you give it to me? That way I'll kill her by shooting her."

"I don't have any money," Rosette said.

They killed her parents via club and machete that day.

This wound up buying the seven Sebasoni kids another night. "We're tired," the militia said after the two murders. "We'll kill these children tomorrow."

"They killed people each day, Tutsis each day, each minute, it was their work," Rosette remembers.

Like clockwork, the militia indeed returned on April 15. They first coerced another Hutu, a neighbour, into imprisoning Rosette and her siblings in his home, under threat of killing the man's son if he didn't comply.

Then the militia said they had an ethical dilemma. Rosette and Freddy were born in Burundi. Their mother had explained this to her killers before she was snuffed out, in a last-ditch attempt to convince the Interahamwe to spare their lives. Though they were ethnically Tutsi, Rosette and Freddy's birthplace gave the militia some pause as to whether or not the two were covered by their marching orders.

"We're going to study this case. If they're Burundian, we're going to see and we're going to kill them later," the Interahamwe said, but this did not apply to Rosette's five younger sisters.

They killed Consolée, Angélique, Florence, Illuminée, and Jeanne.

When Rosette tells me her parents' fate, it is with the detached, matter-of-fact voice of someone who has had to repeat their horrors far too often. But speaking of her five younger sisters, she cannot keep up the facade. Her voice breaks, and teardrops quietly sneak out. She has had practice with the story, of course, and cries in a disciplined, controlled manner, hiccupping rather than sobbing. "When I think about my parents, I tell myself they were adults," she says between gasps. "But why these children, really?"

The Interahamwe clubbed Consolée, Angélique, Florence, Illuminée, and Jeanne, then threw them, still alive, into a nearby septic tank. "They were screaming, they were calling us," says Rosette … until she heard them no more.

Rosette and Freddy agreed that evening they had to find a means of escape. What they devised is cartoonishly simple on paper: pretend they were going to the outhouse and not return. Rosette left first, followed by her brother. Before they fled, each walked back to the home and closed its doors by pushing them in from the outside, mimicking the noise they would make if they had actually stepped in through the threshold and pulled them shut instead.

For the next two weeks, their lives were an ambulatory nightmare. They hid in the bushes by day and dared move only by night, sometimes tripping over corpses they could not see in the darkness.

For garments, they made do by snatching clean laundry off of clotheslines and leaving their dirty attire behind. To feed themselves, they would often pick fruits off of trees.

"We went through all of Rwanda because we didn't know where to go," Rosette says, adding she finds it incredible the pair survived their ordeal at all.

"If there was a house that wasn't finished, or we saw there was nobody there, we would go into it and spend a day there," she says.

They also had just enough cash on them to sometimes duck into a store and buy food and drink before quickly disappearing again, but that got them into trouble once. "We went into a market to buy tea and a few donuts to eat," Rosette recalls, and they were spotted by Interahamwe.

The latter insisted on seeing the Sebasonis' identity cards. The paperwork identifies its holder as either Hutu or Tutsi. Rosette and Freddy had thrown theirs away as soon as they'd escaped, a decision that immediately cast suspicion about them. No Hutu would have had a reason for throwing their documentation away.

The siblings ran, chased by the militia, and managed to get away. Rosette and Freddy found temporary shelter when they reached the Zone Turquoise in the country's southwest, that swath of land guarded by the French army under a U.N. mandate as a haven for fleeing refugees. It has long been controversial — the Tutsi rebels at the time said France's government was striving to help Hutu militia who were fleeing the Tutsis as much as to help the Tutsi victims themselves — but for the Sebasonis, it represented a short break.

They had lived in the region during Rosette's early childhood, and she and Freddy now negotiated a place to stay at her old school, the École Agri-Vétérinaire Kaduha. Here, too, they faced an awful, daily reminder they could be targeted at any time: the school grounds had been improvised into a graveyard for dead Tutsis, and Rosette and Freddy were made to help bury them. "It was like it was our job," Rosette explains. The bodies could have easily been those of her own family members, she says.

Soon, though, came another, greater omen. Rosette says EAV Kaduha also hosted Interahamwe militia running from Tutsi rebels.

"They always threatened my brother," she says. Freddy took it in stride as best he could, until, one day, he discovered a knife in his bed. "He didn't sleep that night," Rosette says. "He came to tell me he thought that was his last day, that he was being followed."

Freddy ditched the school and spent one day with Chadian U.N. peacekeepers. His would-be killers did not find him.

Then he and Rosette left their precarious sanctuary and resumed running.

As the Rwanda Patriotic Front — the Tutsi rebels — successfully installed a new government, putting an end to the genocide, Rosette and Freddy flitted between relatives and family acquaintances. Eventually, they settled with a friend who officially adopted them, and stayed into their adult years.

Sebasoni has become very much a public face of the Interahamwes' horrid legacy. Her testimony is available to anyone who can use a search engine, and she has spent years musing about crimes against humanity.

"The genocide that happened in Rwanda was really unique," she says. "It's different than others because we were killed by our neighbours."

In the energy and excitement that is daily life in the capital, nobody has much time to dwell on this, she says, but venture outside Kigali and you'll see.

Sebasoni says she confronted one of the people who killed her parents herself just six months ago. "It wasn't me," she says the perpetrator told her, saying he was part of a larger group but did not directly partake in their murder.

"I took something," he told her. "I took a wardrobe from your parents," he said. "I'll pay you back."

Rosette walked away from the meeting disappointed she was unable to receive a confession and an apology.

"If they're frank and they tell me the truth and I see that they recognize what they've done," Sebasoni says, "then I would forgive them, because I want to move on, as well."

"I would forgive them all," she says, when I push to see if she is also capable of it for those who took the lives of her five sisters.

"It's in my personal interest, too," she says, "not for me but for my children and my grandchildren."

"We want a country where parents do not intoxicate their children with these genocidal ideas," she says. On that scale between justice and revenge, it is obvious where Rosette's views fit. "Otherwise it's going to continue, it's going to be a vicious circle, vengeance," she adds.

I reflect on what this means for Armenians and Turks as I listen to her words.

The wounds left by the Armenian genocide, with no forgiveness granted by the victims and none asked by the perpetrators, have festered for nearly a century. In Rwanda, it's only been a fifth of that time, yet that's already proven long enough to transmit memories of grievances to the next generation.

Some Armenians now living in the diaspora are still so incensed they say they will never set foot inside Turkey, though they know that means they will never see their ancestral homeland with their own eyes.

Sebasoni wants the hatred to stop, but is worried that won't happen as long as killers keep talking about petty furniture theft rather than those they killed.

She says Interahamwe executioners tend to loosen their tongues when they suspect there are no survivors left from any of the families they butchered, as that way they have only the justice system to worry about, not vigilante revenge.

Many will only get community work if they are found guilty, not time behind bars. "If you say you're going to imprison those who commit genocide, you're going to imprison all of Rwanda," Rosette says.

After she is done with her story, I deliver The Lecture to Rosette anyway. It turns out she is familiar with the broad strokes of the Armenian genocide. It shouldn't surprise me. After all, she has collaborated closely with the centre in Kigali, which does feature panels about the events of 1915.

So absorbed are we in the conversation neither of us pays attention to the darkening clouds outside my window. We return to the hostel's doors, and watch an epic thunderstorm scatter everyone hanging about outside. "I wish I had an umbrella," I tell Rosette. I don't favour them much as I inevitably end up forgetting them somewhere.

"I've got an umbrella," another hostel guest, sitting on a couch, informs us cheerfully, and passes it along.

I open it up, and Rosette and I run outside Discover back to her workplace, laughing as we're soaked. The tiny umbrella is barely large enough for Sebasoni, let alone the both of us, so I mostly use it to cover her until we reach her doorstep.

"You're so wet!" she says, when she has a chance to turn around and sees me dripping head to toe.

It seems unbecoming to complain about a bit of water to someone who's just told you she lived as a fugitive for months after her family was slaughtered.

We both laugh. I shrug it off, thanking her for her time.

When I return to Discover, I also express gratitude to the man who'd lent us his umbrella, as he stares at the rain trailing off my clothes. "She's quite dry," I explain, assuring him his kindness wasn't completely in vain.

Chapter 8

The Strangest Birthday

In April 1994, twenty-five-year-old Jeannette Renzaho welcomed her third child into the world at their home in Kamonyi, some thirty-seven kilometres southwest of Kigali. Her husband, anxious to meet his newborn daughter, hopped into a Red Cross vehicle and sped over from his business in the capital.

But the barriers on the way were too numerous and he never made it back to his wife. Instead of introducing her girl to her father, Jeannette learned from friends she would not see him again.

"After receiving that news, we all knew what was going to happen," Jeannette mused. "We were all sure the Tutsis were going to die."

* * *

She had a few moments of peace to spend with her newborn, then was quickly separated from her two older children.

She fell into the hands of the Interahamwe and was repeatedly sexually assaulted. "There were too many people on me."

When they were satisfied she was dead, Jeannette was thrown into the river.

"I fell into the river," Jeannette Renzaho said. "I didn't drown," she added, telling me and Elvis her story in a Kigali health centre for women with AIDS. Jeannette Renzaho, is, of course, an alias. I'm withholding her real name to protect her dignity.

"I fell on corpses," she said. "Corpses blocked me."

She emerged on shore, her newborn stuck to her back. "I fed her rainwater," Jeannette said. She could not lactate.

A kindly stranger took her in, sheltering her briefly from her nightmare.

*   *   *

It's January 2012. My travels are still months away, plans half-formed, contacts not yet established, and visas not obtained.

My assignment editor at CBC Montreal calls me at home and asks me not to show up at the newsroom for a briefing, but rather to head straight to a local branch of the Federal Court of Appeal. There, I am to meet my camera-person at the door and enter to cover the deportation hearing for Léon Mugesera, the "spokesman of hatred."

A taxi rushes me through the slushy, snowy streets of Montreal as I look up background information about Mugesera on my mobile phone.

This is not the first time the Canadian government has tried handing him back to Rwanda, but so far he has successfully fought against it.

Excerpts of his alleged hatred-inciting speech, which earned him his unflattering moniker, float around online. In 1992, two years before the machetes fell, Mugesera allegedly urged their sharpening, calling the Tutsis "inyenzi" (Kinyarwanda for cockroaches) that had to be crushed, and urging fellow Hutus to toss their bodies into rivers.

The man who emerges from a car and is escorted into the three-floor cream-coloured building, past the handful of snowy stairs at the entrance, looks a far cry from the monster who could spit such inflammatory rhetoric. He is tall (as tall as a Tutsi, some would mention with irony), but bent, perhaps by the effort of fighting his forced transfer to Kigali. Round spectacles, a greying and thinning hairline and goatee lend him the air of an avuncular professor. And he walks with a limp and a cane.

He pivots and grins feebly this way and that at the news cameras waiting in the court lobby for their precious few seconds of footage. He says not a word, though, dodging the scores of audio recorders and microphones brandished toward him as he disappears in and out of the hearing room. His lawyer, too, keeps his words for the judge.

Mugesera earns himself another brief respite. It would be closer to the end of the month before he would be evicted.

Returning to the newsroom, I find a home number for a "Mugesera" in Quebec City. It's a rare family name in Canada. Find one in a directory and it's likely you've found him, or at least someone who is related. Fingers trembling, I punch in the digits on the well-worn buttons of the phone at my desk and listen to the ring tone. The connection carries my voice not only a physical distance but ninety-seven years back through time. The man who is going to answer may as well be among those who slaughtered my kin.

There's no pickup.

I am reassigned to a different story, and I keep his in the back of my head.

* * *

It is the morning of May 8, 2012, and I'm attending a genocide reconciliation workshop at the Kigali Memorial Centre.

Some thirty students from schools across Kigali sit on wooden chairs in a sunlit room, listening to two bright, energetic lecturers. Elvis and I remain in the back, and he occasionally whispers translations to me.

The lecturers, too, are sometimes polite enough to sneak English sound bites into their lessons. "Mistaken understandings can create misinformed decisions," one tells his students, having them repeat the statement.

Then they briefly hush the room to play an audio clip. It is a shrill excerpt from what sounds like a public speech in Kinyarwanda. Fewer than forty seconds elapse before one of the lecturers clicks the stop button and asks his students if they recognize the voice.

"Mugesera," the group whispers in quasi-unanimity.

* * *

It is the evening of May 8, 2012, and I'm sitting on Discover Rwanda's deck planning tomorrow's agenda, which includes Léon Mugesera's pre-trial hearing.

"Happy birthday, man," René Wollenschein amicably interrupts in front of a group of people, having gleaned the information off of Facebook, that ubiquitous over-sharer.

"We should celebrate," says Marlene, who is staying at Discover for a spell and happens to overhear.

We soon have a litany of excuses for celebrating. René says this is his last night in Kigali. Marlene says she has just confirmed via email the date of her university graduation ceremony. Another girl, Kate Zhu from Singapore, who has joined in on our conversation, explains her own birthday was four days earlier.

We walk over to a Chinese restaurant nearby. Evidently, it's already a little too chilly for anyone except the Canadian, as my three friends all toss light jackets on, the open zipper of René's still showing his toothy pendant.

A waitress sits us around a red table, walling us from the rest of the clientele in a fenced booth. We place our orders, René sticking to spring rolls as he insists he is not hungry. I ask for beef and rice, and Marlene a bowl of sweet and sour soup.

When everyone's food arrives, it's clear we'll have to share. Marlene's bowl is nearly bottomless, and whereas René insists he has no need of a full meal, certainly the single, short, stick-figure of a roll that greets him won't do.

As we split all of our dishes, René and Kate amuse themselves and us by using some of the condiments and food on the table to create a couple of clown-like faces on their plates. Kate's has rather thick, frowning eyebrows.

"It's an angry Armenian clown," I proclaim, alluding to the twin hairy bars brooding atop my own peepers.

* * *

The next morning, May 9, Elvis and I attend Léon Mugesera's first pre-trial session. There's a lineup to enter the packed courtroom at Rwanda's Tribunal de Grande Instance on the outskirts of Kigali.

It's not only locals who are here to fill the seats and satisfy their curiosity. Sigall Horovitz, a friendly law professor I met

Accused génocidaire Léon Mugesera sitting in a courtroom on the outskirts of Kigali during his pre-trial proceedings.

through a connection, has brought over her class from Hebrew University of Jerusalem in Israel.

Léon Mugesera shows up, looking sicklier still than he did in Montreal in January.

In a lively hot pink shirt and a wrinkled grey suit, he pleads he is too ill to stand trial. He also demands access to his entire dossier, explaining he has been given only the first ten pages.

The prosecution will have none of it, saying Mugesera has the exact documents he's asked for, and it has obtained a medical report from the accused's own doctor showing he is not too weak to stand trial.

Again I look at the meek fellow and make an effort to see him calling for rivers filled with blood.

* * *

It is day two of Mugesera's pre-trial court proceedings. He appears wearing the same hot pink shirt and wrinkled grey suit he had yesterday.

The hearing is brief. The judge disagrees on his being unfit to stand trial, and says he will be given access to the documents he needs to prepare.

* * *

Jeannette Renzaho's sanctuary lasted only so long. Unmoved by the pity that swayed the man who sheltered her, she says, a relative of his forced her out of the home.

Jeannette had nowhere to turn, and no idea what fate had befallen her two older children. She could only assume they were dead.

Soon she fell again into the hands of the Interahamwe. "They did whatever they wanted with me," she said. "Whoever wanted to see a naked woman, and wanted to take my clothes off as they wished, whoever wanted to sleep with a woman, came to do that with me," she said. "I was like their toy."

* * *

Before attending the reconciliation workshop, one student tells me, she had very little idea of what the genocide actually was.

"I thought they were simple killings," she says shyly during a quick interview following the day's lecture.

Much the same for another student, Justin Niyonkuru, seventeen. "We didn't talk about it with our parents," he says. "They don't even talk about it. I couldn't ask them," he says.

*   *   *

Maybe reconciliation is not a pipe dream. Maybe it's not too abstract a concept for these children who barely know about the genocide. After all, the survivors I meet at the AIDS health centre say they've managed to forgive, though it's often through tears and in long, reflective pauses between bits of telling their stories that they say so. During one such break, a hand pushes the meeting room's wooden door open just a crack, throws a box of napkins on the table, much to the relief of me and Elvis, and disappears again, shutting the door.

Thérèse Bemeriki (real name also withheld) was thirty-eight years old in 1994. She lost everyone except her kid brother, and the details of how she wound up a patient at the health centre are too painful for her to share.

"Among the people who killed my family are some who stayed at my house," she tells me. "I see them. When I'm sick, they visit me, when I have a problem, they visit me. When they have a problem, I also go see them. I forget everything."

There is another who looks more for justice than revenge.

*   *   *

Jeannette Renzaho was saved from her tormentors when the RPF troops arrived on the scene in 1994. And she again encountered the man who had briefly sheltered her.

Gently, slowly, he told her he had some important news. The good kind, he said, when asked to elaborate, but did not dare tell her more. He then took her with him, and brought her to her two older children, still breathing.

"They were in terrible condition, but they were alive," she said.

Chapter 9

Facing the Music

On the evening of May 11, Kate Zhu and I decide to hang out back at Discover with some new visitors at the hostel, in part because they all seem so nice and eager to make friends, in part because our other friends have already packed their bags … and, in part, I suspect, because human contact and interaction are important after spending the better part of the day visiting skulls, bones, and tattered, bloody rags. The two of us had gone to see two memorial sites outside of Kigali during the day.

We all take a walk up the street to the better-stocked bar on one of the top floors of a skyscraper hotel. As it is practically deserted, we have it nearly all to ourselves. We watch the blanket of lights on Kigali's teeming hills through the room's great bay windows as the sun disappears.

Three of the others stand out to me, each of them representing an aspect of my own trip — and if I'm to be honest — arguably pulling it off better.

One, from the United States, is travelling through Africa. To my story of venturing alone through what I'd like to tell myself is an impressive journey, he tells that his is a land trip through several countries. With an all-American football player's build and swagger, he alludes to Sudan as one of the many places on his odyssey as if it were no big deal, though I suspect that's likely to be the case for most people out for a little bit of tourism, not trying to remind the world of more than four hundred thousand dead Darfuris.

Still, he's doing it all on a bad-ass motorcycle. I don't know much about bikes, but atop his, he looks like he could handle both the non-existent road network between the desert refugee camps of Chad and the mountainous jungle refuge of the Amahoro near Kinigi with no trouble, probably enjoying the challenge.

Another is in town from Darwin, Australia. To my story of meeting genocide survivors and compassionately listening to their testimonies, he raises the fact he actually sponsors two orphans in Rwanda, and is here to check on them.

And the quietest of all is a freelance photographer who wants to make his way into the DRC, specifically an area caught in a firefight between militias everyone else is running away from.

In a couple of days I will fly to Turkey, where the paranoid Armenian in me sees himself refused entry upon landing at the Istanbul Atatürk Airport, or, worse, the subject of a quiet arrest and detainment in some dank hole. My nervousness about flying to the tourist hotspot that is Istanbul admittedly seems a little childish in comparison to the suffering of the genocide victims I have spoken to in Rwanda, but the photographer understands where I'm coming from.

"Play it cool," he says, and, "you'll be fine," his serenity and shoulder-length brown hair and beard lending him the airs of an actor auditioning for the next cinematic adaptation of the New Testament.

* * *

The next night, my last in Kigali, I'm sipping banana wine on the deck of the Discover Rwanda, as I chat of genocide and massacres with an Austrian friend I've met over the last couple of days.

He's tasting banana beer. We purchased the beverages at a nearby grocery store, both realizing we were about to leave the country and had yet to taste a couple of its more popular drinks.

He believes the Armenian genocide will never be recognized by Turkey if it doesn't happen in the next couple of generations. It is simply a matter of time, for him. Having listened to The Lecture (hey, he's the one who asked me the reason for my travels, I did not mean to subject him to it), he concludes that my own children and grandchildren, if I ever have any, just will not have the same emotional attachment as I do to the events of 1915. Already, he says, I care a lot less than my parents do. That would explain the transcontinental journey. Forgive and forget.

I rebuff my friend's assertion that I care less than my parents by explaining, for what feels the umpteenth time, my backstory.

He makes all of his points succinctly, with an almost preternatural cool and calm I'm not sure I've seen anyone keep when debating as volatile a matter as crimes against humanity. At over six feet tall, he's certainly self-assured enough, which may explain why he does not think he needs to raise his voice.

At any rate, either he doesn't see it, or he's too much of a gentleman to point out how my family history might easily validate his first argument: that my own offspring would not carry this kind of baggage and therefore be less likely to care.

"You sure know how to pick them," he says instead in allusion to the countries the Boudjikanians have lived in and escaped from so far, chuckling through his well-trimmed, curly, reddish beard.

I sense he would apply his point about the futility of an individual pushing for recognition on a larger, national scale, for all of Armenia, too.

But I bite my tongue and do not delve into how it would be extremely difficult for the modern country, also, to forget about the importance of genocide recognition.

A landlocked, tiny nation, its largest border is with Turkey, and that remains completely shut. The two states have no diplomatic relations to speak of. Armenia continues to press the issue of 1915's deaths, and Turkey vehemently continues to deny the genocide.

Modern Armenians living in the country all know no small part of its economic difficulties are because of the shut border. Forgetting the root cause of it all seems unlikely.

*   *   *

In a thinly wooded area some twenty-five kilometres south of Kigali stands Ntamara. In 1994, refugees flocked to this Catholic church.

But no fear of God held the Interahamwe back.

There are few human remains at the Ntamara site nowadays. Bodies have been taken out of the building. The government, however, has left the clothes of victims behind. Silent testimony to what happened here, they're piled up on the pews, all blood-stained.

Ntamara's "twin," Nyamata, is just as grim. And here, behind its red brick walls, Kate Zhu and I are alone to contemplate the history, unlike at Ntamara, which happened to be full of other visitors upon our arrival.

The insides and pews of Nyamata, too, are decorated with the victims' apparel, illuminated by stark sunlight falling in through the structure's square-paneled windows. It's estimated about ten thousand civilians were killed around this site alone. That's about a hundredth of those killed during the entire genocide.

Here I see a child's turquoise blouse; there, a hat atop a mound of shirts.

Nyamata is less timid about exposing its visitors to the blunt horrors of the killings. Rows of skulls are preserved behind glass showcases in a basement area outside the church. I spot one with an extra hole, another that looks crushed. It reminds me of the genocide memorial housed in the Armenian Church Catholicosate at Antelias, near Beirut, a seat of the Armenian Apostolic Church.

Nyamata houses boxes adorned with crosses, too. You wouldn't immediately deduce they were coffins: they don't look the right shape. But a guard assures us that's the case. Each holds many bodies.

Italian aid worker Tonia Locatelli's tomb at the Nyamata memorial site in Rwanda.

Outside, we see one more gravestone, that of Italian aid worker Tonia Locatelli. She is remembered for her dire warnings to foreign governments and media, a voice raging against the impending darkness two years before it fully fell.

In 1992, the world heard of the first massacres through Locatelli. She was killed on March 9 of that year. In 1994, nearly a million people died.

My Austrian friend confesses he has a difficult time putting himself in the shoes of survivors or their descendants. "My ancestors were on the other end of the stick," he says.

He reveals his grandfather, whom he never met, was a Nazi. I ask if this bothers him.

"Everyone was a Nazi," he shrugs. It's a fair point about Second World War Austria. Why should he be made to feel guilty about it fifty years later?

As I drift off to sleep that night, the words come back to me. Would some modern-day Turks have the same indifference toward what their ancestors did, for the same reason?

The sticking points, again, are acknowledgement and forgiveness. The world at large recognizes the Nazis' crimes, and the successors to those regimes have repented. Not so with Turkey.

Chapter 10

The G Word

It is afternoon, Friday, January 19, 2007. At the offices of the bilingual Turkish-Armenian weekly *Agos*, in Istanbul's posh Osman Bey district, ethnic Armenian editors Sarkis Seropyan and Hrant Dink complete their editorial meeting, deciding on priorities for the next issue.

It's a well-worn ritual for the two old colleagues, who are used to then retreating to their separate quarters and plugging ahead on the forthcoming paper. After all, it has to go to press by next Wednesday, which means they must squeeze in some work before Saturday, or face dealing with more on their plate Monday.

It's been about a week since Dink, a vocal proponent of genocide recognition in Turkey, has publicly mused about anonymous death threats he's received. Seropyan walks upstairs to his office. An odd commotion reaches him from street-level. He hears what sound like screams. Voices he recognizes, too: the newspaper's accountants and cook. He rushes downstairs.

When Seropyan emerges on the street, the deed is done. Dink, with whom he'd ended a meeting moments ago, is lying sprawled on the sidewalk, shot, bleeding to death.

* * *

It is May 14, 2012. Turkey's attempt at seducing me begins far before I land in the country. Staff aboard the Turkish Airlines flight from Ethiopia are polite and courteous; my seat exceedingly comfortable. This is the first plane I've sat on in nearly a month that doesn't ask me to help ensure passenger safety in the event of an emergency — a nice bonus.

Then there's the food. With Turkey's geographical proximity to, and geopolitical influence over, both Lebanon and Armenia, it's closer to my mom's cooking than typical airplane fare.

Instead of a glorified PowerPoint presentation, the safety video is a cheesy though entertaining Three Stooges–esque short starring members of the Manchester United soccer club, draped in the colours of the Turkish flag. Of course, how closely people follow the instructions rather than laugh along at the Da Silva brothers stripping Wayne Rooney of his captain's cap may be a bit of a question, but I digress.

The attractiveness of my flight is further enhanced by the fact that my entertainment options include an animated superhero movie. If I'm about to get arrested and detained, I tell myself, I may as well watch Batman running around Gotham City first.

In Istanbul, following a brief difficulty finding my luggage at the crowded airport, and a rather long lineup to purchase my tourist visa, I continue to be wooed. The city's large, densely populated streets remind me of major European capitals. The familiar mixes with the strange: in Turkish, it is the Yenilmezer, not the Avengers, who will be uniting to save the world from an extraterrestrial threat at a movie multiplex near you this summer, as advertised by omnipresent posters plastered all over building walls. Large fishing rods arc over the Bosporus Strait, men and women waiting patiently for a tug.

As I stroll by its shores, a young shoe shiner insists on giving my footwear a rub, promising a great discount as he loves dealing with tourists. I politely decline and keep walking, despite his protestations and the patches of dull grey beginning to poke through the veneer of my black leathers.

Eventually, he walks ahead of me, and, glancing furtively behind his shoulder, drops a brush in my path. It's a trick of the trade, according to my guidebook: get the good Samaritan traveller to pick it up, lose yourself in endless thank-yous, promise a free shoe-shine job, then remark, dismayed, that you took up too much time or used up too many supplies and request payment anyway. I deliberately circle around the object at the heart of the supposed scam and keep on my way. The shoe shiner, annoyed, turns back and runs past me to grab his brush. With the city's popularity among globetrotters, there's no shortage of people on whom to ply his trade.

Walking on to lush Sultanahmet Square, dominated by both the Blue Mosque and the Ayasofya, with a tramline conveniently snaking by, feels like stepping into history.

That encounter with history and tradition can sometimes be amusing. Grabbing a bite to eat at a restaurant in the shadow of the two mosques one evening, I ask for wine. The waiter looks at me surprised, explaining the eatery's proximity to Muslim places of worship forbids him from serving alcohol. He instead offers a "fantastic" exotic fruit punch, an extra punch on the "fan" syllable when he delivers the word, as if he'd memorized a sales pitch based on Hollywood mannerisms.

For Armenians, though, the encounter with history and tradition can be, equally, discomfiting. Armenians lived in the

Ottoman Empire for centuries. The community in Istanbul numbers just over fifty thousand now, a drastic drop since 1915. The Armenian Apostolic Church has a Patriarchate in the city, one I ask a tourist office clerk to point out on a map for me. The clerk first insists I'm mistaken, and points to Georgian and Greek churches, instead. I assure him there's an Armenian church seat as well. He takes another look at his map, and his disbelief upon finding it suggests he suspects I managed to conjure it through some magic spell. He double-checks on Google before conceding I'm not making anything up.

Istanbul is steeped in history. It has enthroned Roman, Byzantine, and Greek emperors, its people a mix from all over Europe and Asia. The Ottoman Turks conquered the city in 1452, back when it was still known as Constantinople. By then, the Armenians had already long lost their last independent kingdom in the region. Over the next few centuries, wars between greater nations divided the Armenian population. What would have been the eastern part of older Armenian kingdoms wound up in the hands of the Persians, and then the Russians. It is roughly this region that corresponds to the modern independent country of Armenia. What would have been the western part of older Armenia, where my ancestors are from, ended up in the Ottoman Empire.

To my delight, I discover a secret part of Istanbul's past all historians seem to have somehow missed. It turns out the city changed hands yet again after it was conquered by the Turks in 1452. It has been taken over by cats.

They run all over the former imperial capital, soaking in the sun by the long Bosporus coast line, enjoying food dished out by locals and tourists alike in places such as Gülhane, the cliff-top public park surrounding Topkapi Palace. Once the primary residence of Ottoman sultans, it is closed for

Istanbul basically belongs to the cats.

renovations on the day I make it to the golden arches of its gates, so I have to make do just watching the furballs.

A handful of felines live happily inside my hotel, a converted Turkish bath house, vines growing over its brown, seventeenth-century walls.

I arrive at Empress Zoe right on time for the delicious buffet breakfast. "Is this yogourt?" I ask a hotel worker incredulously, pointing at a large bowl that could hardly be anything else. He laughs and nods. Besides one Rwandan morning's experience of biting too enthusiastically into a bowl of cereal flooded with expired milk, I have not touched dairy since leaving Canada.

As I sit down to eat in the airy, busy courtyard, I'm joined by a tiny, white-and-beige tabby that quietly hops on the chair across and observes without a single mew. To my surprise, it's happy to let me pat its head and stroke the underside of its chin without making any overt motions asking for grub. If this is the infamous Turkish secret service apparatus come to spy on me, it's doing a heck of a job.

I relax in the cozy reception area, on a plush old couch, while waiting for the hotel to prepare my room. A chunkier specimen of feline, a ginger-coloured veteran with a battle scar from some secret street fight across one of its emerald eyes, curls up next to me and decides it's a good spot for a nap after a round of kneading on my jeans. Another tourist walks by, delighted at the scene, and asks for my permission to take a picture. I oblige, and she smiles in delight as she points her SLR camera at me to fire away. Maybe her shot is what ends up in the hands of the secret service, who knows.

*   *   *

A shy, friendly young woman agrees to help me make my way through Istanbul's byzantine subway system, explaining she is headed for the same stop. "Come wizz me," she says with an accent as we reach our station, and leads me to the exit I need before going her separate way.

Unease starts seriously creeping in when I arrive near the *Agos* office, a short walk from the subway.

I've come in the run-up to the Atatürk Youth and Sports Day commemoration, a big Turkish holiday. Buildings in Istanbul are covered in large, red-and-white flags, and banners of iconic figures from the country's history.

A poster of national hero Mustafa Kemal Atatürk droops over *Agos*. Stylishly dressed in a dark suit jacket against a charcoal grey backdrop, he also has a white napkin folded neatly in his breast pocket to match his shirt. Atatürk looks solemn, lips pursed in a tight line underneath a blondish handlebar moustache, much of his hair hidden by a black hat, its edges and shape lost in the non-descript background. A red tie, further linking the image to the colours of Turkish patriotism, completes the look. Behind him, the *Agos* building, with its man-high windows, ornamental sculptures jutting out atop their frames, is hidden from view. A handful of ground-floor boutiques with no relation to the newspaper are all that peek out underneath Kemal.

Atatürk is, to say the least, a controversial figure for Armenians. Though the father of modern Turkey did not directly have a hand in planning the genocide, and went as far as to refer to the massacres as a "shameful act," he later also became the first in a long line of Turkish statesmen to minimize their scale. Before heading the Turkish National Movement, the political party that would give birth to the Republic of Turkey as it is known today, he was a member of the Committee for Union and Progress, the very same party that devised the annihilation of Armenians. There were also direct ties between some of the men who surrounded him in his government and the events of 1915. Topal Osman, a militia leader responsible for some of the massacres, became commander of Kemal's special bodyguard regiment. Ali Cenani Bey, who supervised some deportations as a parliamentary deputy of the Ottoman Empire during the First World War, served as minister of trade and commerce under Atatürk.

At the foot of *Agos* lies another highly charged symbol, a plaque commemorating the exact spot Dink was assassinated, in both Turkish and Armenian. Latin and Armenian letters are formed in white across its black surface. Dink, who advocated dialogue with the Turks as he called for recognition of the Armenian genocide, was gunned down for his efforts by a seventeen-year-old boy. Ogün Samast was quickly arrested. Almost as quickly, a picture was leaked of him, a police officer, and a security guard standing next to each other, wearing grim smiles as the young man held the Turkish flag unfolded in half-outstretched arms. Exactly who was behind Samast remains a mystery for authorities and judiciary to investigate, although Dink's family lawyers have maintained

Mustafa Kemal Atatürk and the Turkish flag cover nearly the whole of Turkish-Armenian newspaper Agos's office building on the day I visit.

for years there was more to it than a wanton act of violence by a misguided teen. Fethiye Çetin and Cem Halavurt say Dink was a target of the ultranationalist group Ergenekon. Thirty-three of its alleged members were arrested about a year after the journalist's death in an unrelated matter, inciting armed revolt against the government. It took up much more space in Turkish media.

There was outrage both in Turkey and abroad following Dink's death. As I stare at the square on the sidewalk, I recall the "We are all Hrant Dink" protest placards I had read of in international coverage focused on the streets of Istanbul. I also recall the "We are all Rwandan" cries I heard echoing

A plaque commemorating Turkish-Armenian journalist Hrant Dink. In English it would read "Hrant Dink was killed here on January 19, 2007, at 3:05 p.m."

in a movie fictionalizing a dramatic post-genocide encounter between Interahamwe remnants and the poor students they would have gunned down, shown in the reconciliation workshop in Kigali.

Above me Atatürk looms tall over where Dink breathed his last.

*   *   *

The heavy wrought-iron gates and doors and the brick interiors of the *Agos* building remind me of my childhood's Beirut apartments, particularly my grandfather's place. I spend little time at the paper on my first visit, just enough to ask staff their opinion of the banner decorating their office. They explain they went home one evening, returned the next day, and found it draped there, put up with no prior warning. And so they have had to live with it, with little choice but to shrug it off as coincidence. In the busy newsroom bullpen, its large wooden desks cluttered with the piles of paperwork that tend to accumulate on many a journalist's work space, I spend a few minutes waiting to arrange an interview with Sarkis Seropyan, now the paper's Armenian-language section editor. I'm astonished as I am introduced to an ethnic Armenian writer at the paper who doesn't speak a word of the language, probably more so than he is surprised to meet somebody who can't communicate with him in Turkish. For many diaspora Armenians, it would be unthinkable to meet someone of Armenian descent who doesn't speak their culture's mother tongue, but fully functions in Turkish.

As they retell the story of the genocide to their children, Armenians often cite mothers desperately scratching the long, curvaceous letters of the centuries-old Armenian alphabet in the desert sands during 1915's death marches, a bid to have their offspring never forget the language. It is, perhaps, a difficult truth to verify, more symbol than fact, but good luck ridding your mind of such a powerful, archetypal image after listening to its description since you were knee-high.

In fact, one of our more famous poets, the late Silva Kaputikyan, who was born shortly after the genocide, urges in one work for Armenian sons to always remember the tongue, though they may forget their mothers.

For many Armenians, the idea of linguistic amnesia has become inexorably intertwined with the idea of forgetting the genocide. Another of our famous poets, Avedis Aharonian, wrote that the world should condemn Armenians if they ever fail to remember the horrors they suffered in 1915. In songs sung around campfires in places as far-flung from Armenia and each other as Canada and Australia, diaspora Armenian scouts hum along about how they are few in number but remain Armenian, and do not forget their mother tongue.

Yet in Istanbul, where Turkish is the lingua franca, it cannot be that uncommon for ethnic Armenians to focus on speaking that language instead of their ancestral one. How could you get by without an ability to understand, read, and write the country's official speech?

My mind tells me not to be bothered by the idea the polite man cannot return my *parev* ("Hello," in my native language), but my years of upbringing in a relatively sheltered environment somewhat resist this rational point of view. I do not know if it is my interlocutor's youth that bothers me so. He may be the only person in the room besides me with no grey hair, and is also the only person who cannot speak Armenian. After trying in vain to engage me in Turkish, he walks off back to his work, ever a gracious smile on his lips.

Seropyan has the body language of a newsman trying to meet deadlines, mostly staring at his computer monitor while he tersely agrees to make some time for me on the next day.

* * *

It is night and I'm returning to the hotel after dinner as Istanbul rolls by my streetcar.

The car is nearly deserted. One man sits across from me, and several benches away are two others, in their twenties, chattering in Turkish. Well, one is doing the chattering, the other mostly just listens. The talker looks like an athlete, muscled arms peeking through a tight green T-shirt; long, dirty blond hair falls onto his back from underneath a dark baseball cap.

We are still a ways from my stop when they decide on a whim to approach me. The listener sits immediately to my left, the athlete faces him. They essentially bracket me between themselves and the window.

They continue speaking to each other.

I think about the odds of my not getting lost by night if I jump off the tram at an incorrect stop in a city where I've spent fewer than twenty-four hours.

Their body language betrays no attempt at watching me. Then again, if they were good spies, it wouldn't.

At a rare intervention of listener, athlete reaches into his sports bag and retrieves a lighter. He flicks it on a couple of times, bounces and twists it between his fingertips with a practised lack of effort.

I think of Armenians torched in the caves of Der El Zor.

Listener says something again. Athlete, laughing, passes

him the lighter. I can hear the Armenians screaming. The lighter is right next to me now, as listener calmly observes it.

A couple of rowdy youths playing with fire on public transit seems like a strange way for the secret service to intimidate you, but I've been more paranoid before.

The amateur action hero in me starts building contingencies. Listener doesn't look that tough. Should he appear to brandish that lighter at me, I could easily knock it out of his fingers.

Athlete, sitting smugly across, could be more of a problem. But, strong as he looks, I bet a shove of my heavy backpack on his chest could still knock him back long enough for me to … to what, exactly?

The streetcar's doors are shut. Unless I happen to be at a stop as they make their move, or push my hypothetical stunt to the point of trying to jump through glass, I'm not going anywhere.

And all this planning has yet to factor in the third man who'd been across from me since the beginning of the ride, seemingly oblivious to the people around him.

Athlete, ever with the arrogant laugh, snatches the lighter back from listener.

We get to my station.

When I rise, clutching my bag, both politely pull themselves back to let me exit.

* * *

It was Dink's death that briefly and brightly drew much of the international media's spotlight on him, but he and *Agos* had already been making waves in Turkey.

In his grave monotone, Dink's collaborator Sarkis Seropyan explains how it started when the pair of them, along with Dink's son, Arat, then acting editor at the paper, were dragged to court for "insulting Turkishness." Seropyan's small, deep-set eyes observe me from behind the glasses resting on the bridge of his wide nose, from underneath his bushy, snowy, thunder cloud–like eyebrows. The latter are a sharp departure from his vanishing grey hairline in their permanent marker–like thickness.

How exactly did the three men attract the ire of the Turkish judiciary? In 2006, the news agency Reuters asked Hrant Dink if the events of 1915 constituted genocide. Seropyan quotes his late friend's answer to me as follows: "Two million Armenians lived in this country before 1915. After 1915 that number went down to three hundred thousand. Today it is at sixty thousand. You decide whether or not this can be called genocide."

And that, as they say, was that. Seropyan says Turkish media across the country declared Dink was officially calling the events genocide. A few days later, *Agos* followed suit.

All this runs afoul of the Turkish penal code, specifically Article 301, which makes it a crime to mention the possibility Turks may have committed genocide, as an affront to the very idea of being Turkish.

But the law is enforced only if someone complains to the courts. And of course, *Agos* staff found themselves the subjects of such a complaint.

Dinks Senior and Junior, along with Seropyan, were arraigned. Hrant Dink would never live to see a verdict. In October 2007, a mere ten months after he was assassinated, his son Arat and Seropyan were found guilty and each handed a one-year suspended sentence.

They did not have to serve the time, Seropyan explains, since the Turkish legal system allowed them to walk away because this was the first-ever blemish on their records. Were they found guilty of something else, on another occasion, the time would be compounded.

Their conviction was stayed, however, and the case was eventually thrown out of court. According to Seropyan, Article 301 is a very special piece of legislation. Any tribunal that wishes to charge people under it must seek permission from the Turkish justice minister himself.

Through some bureaucratic fluke, this was not done in the case of Seropyan and the Dinks. They were called forward and asked if they wished to be tried again.

"The natural thing to do would have been to say 'No, we don't wish to be tried again,'" Seropyan says.

They, however, went the opposite route, wanting to ensure their names were cleared once and for all. In fact, the justice minister would not end up granting permission for the trial to take place, and so they did not appear before the courts again.

Article 301 never did silence Hrant Dink. Bullets in the back of his head would have to do that, instead.

"Hrant Dink was not only among the paper's founders, but its main editor … its everything," Seropyan says, still devastated five years later. "The killing of Hrant Dink left us, from one moment to the next, in a state of emptiness for a while."

It's hard not to envision how differently the geopolitics of genocide recognition would be playing out at the dawn of the one-hundredth anniversary if as outspoken a proponent as Hrant Dink were still alive.

That idea must haunt the *Agos* office every day. Seropyan broaches the subject himself, with no question from me. Perhaps he can tell one is on the tip of my tongue.

"We're the children of a people who have sacrificed so many," Seropyan declares Dink would repeatedly say. "But we

Poet Daniel Varoujan's bust at the Armenian cemetery in Istanbul's Sisli district. Varoujan was brutally slaughtered during the Armenian genocide.

love our country. This is our birthplace, this is our country, we have to untie this knot, we have to sit down and come to a bilateral agreement [with the Turks]."

But this is possible only after the government acknowledges the past; and since that has yet to occur, the paper, despite its brush with 301, hasn't watered down its provocative editorials.

I ask Seropyan how he remains so unafraid.

"Who says I'm not afraid?" he laughs bitterly. Since his own appearance at the courts, Seropyan says, he has sold his ownership shares in the paper. Thus, he cannot be held liable for the words of others. "If I write anything [about the genocide] or not is entirely up to me," he says.

"But have you written [on the issue] since 2007, or not?"

"Who knows, maybe I have written," he says with a cryptic harrumph. "How long can you hide the past, anyway?"

* * *

Buffered from the city noise through tall walls and trees, in Istanbul's Şişli district is its Armenian cemetery, under the shadow of a Trump Tower under construction.

Tombstones recall the names of Armenians who fell, sometimes in that dark year, sometimes not. It feels entirely deserted when I visit, not another soul in sight on the neat, grey asphalt walkways cutting paths through the thickly growing vegetation. Some areas are more jumbled than others, lots and tombstones practically pushing against each other in the crowded struggle for a peaceful final resting place.

A black bust of one of our greatest poets, Daniel Varoujan, is mounted atop a marble slab. The sculptor has given form to one of Varoujan's hands, pensively supporting his chin. When I happen upon it, a single red rose lies on a smaller slab right next to the one bearing the intellectual's likeness.

Varoujan lived only to the age of thirty-one. It is said his was not a quick death. On one of the endless caravans of victims during the genocide, he and other prisoners were stopped by Kurdish mercenaries, robbed, and stripped of their clothes. He and his fellow prisoners were then slowly cut with knives. Varoujan reportedly put up a fight, and had his eyes dug out as recompense.

Near Varoujan, another marble slab, carved with a poem. Not one of his own, evidently it is authored by the man whose grinning, well-coiffed likeness occupies a section of the sculpture. I cannot quite make out his mimicked, scrawled signature. The piece is not one I've heard before, but it speaks to me now:

> In the end, whatever you think on the way, whatever you see, whatever life you live beyond this life, whatever you have there, whatever you hoped to … whatever you hoped was waiting for you, whatever called you, and whatever you found and loved, whatever you wanted, and whatever remained to you from this amazing trip, whatever you did not want to even tell yourself for fear of forgetting, whatever you still carry with you like a question.

* * *

A misty evening rain covers Istanbul's streets as I hastily exit the hotel, searching for an ATM. It's barely past 8:00 p.m., but I've already had dinner and need to fly very early the next morning, so leaving the cash question to tomorrow just won't do.

"Umbrella, sir, my friend, umbrella," a merchant suggests somewhere on a public square nearby. I politely nod without really turning toward him, and keep walking to the ATMs in front of me. Just as I approach, a black car pulls up by my side.

The driver lowers his passenger window. Well-groomed and dressed in a full suit, with a big smile, he rattles off a couple of sentences in Turkish.

"I don't speak Turkish, I'm sorry," I say, concerned he could be a colleague of the two youths on the tramway.

"Ah, it's okay. Where are you from?"

The wheels are nice, and so is the outfit. Rather pricy for a scamming operation. He probably is the government, I tell myself; play nice, just not too nice.

"Canada, Montreal," I reply, hiding behind what is, in this instance, the most harmless third of my identity.

Strictly speaking, it's not a lie. It says Canadian on the passport, and that's what I've been since, if not 1991, then that day four years later, when my Grade 5 homeroom teacher had at first rather indignantly asked under what circumstances my parents had convinced the principal's office I needed to cut class early, and then had proceeded to lead the room in cheerful applause when I'd announced I was to attend a citizenship ceremony.

The accolades had seemed a little unearned. After all, being a minor, all I had to do was be present on the big day. My mother and father had had to do all the heavy lifting, learning about the country's history, economy, and politics to pass the citizenship test.

Appropriately enough, it had snowed on the drive home from the ceremony. By then, the white powdery stuff had lost much of the wonder I'd experienced the first time I'd cast eyes on snow in the school recess yard in '91.

"I guess the snow looks a little more Canadian now," I'd declared rather meaninglessly on citizenship day, looking out the car's backseat window at the flakes fluttering to the ground.

"What does that mean?" my dad had asked, perhaps a little curious but largely just amused. I'm not sure I came up with an answer.

And in Istanbul, the man who did receive an answer remains silent for a while, contemplating its worth.

What is he calculating behind the beaming expression? Ninety per cent sure this is the Armenian guy who is also a journalist from Montreal who's written about the genocide before, I picture his gears turning. I'd penned a couple of pieces in a student publication during my university days, which I'd always half-joked had earned me a spot on some sort of Turkish intelligence watch list.

"Ah, Canada, I have a cousin there, studying, very nice," he says.

Likely story. "You should visit sometime, it's very nice."

Who stops to speak to a total stranger in the middle of the night?

"I'm from southern Turkey, southern Anatolia," he explains. "But now I'm here on conference."

As if I'd asked.

"You're here on work, exhibit?" He continues. I'm not sure if the poor English is just poor English, or if it's because he's a little nervous about hiding his interrogation so thinly.

"I'm just here to see the city, beautiful city," I say.

"Me I'm a cockpit design engineer," he says, showing off the inside of his car with a sweeping hand gesture he could have learned as a stage magician's apprentice.

"That's great, that's a very nice job." *You're not finding out what I do that easily.*

"Where are you staying? I'm at Four Seasons," he says.

"I'm at Empress Zoe, near Four Seasons," I say, stupidly.

"Where are you originally from?" he asks, elevating my suspicion about what he's trying to get at. The Canada explanation is evidently not good enough.

"Lebanon," I end it there, stopping at the second least harmful third of my identity. For once in my life, I keep the laborious "but I'm ethnically Armenian" explanation to myself, and banish any idea at all of delivering The Lecture.

"Ah, ahlen habibi ("hello, friend" in Arabic)," he grins, and shakes my hand. I dimly register this is the second time he's shaking my hand in the space of a minute.

"Come, I go to the Turkish bathhouse for one drink, you come," he says.

I tell him I can't.

"It's on me," he says.

"I don't have the time, flying very early tomorrow," I say, another piece of information I should have kept to myself.

"I understand," he says, but proceeds to open his passenger door. "Come, just one quick drink on me."

"I really can't," I say, and with some trepidation give my thanks and shut the door right back on him. It is probably the rudest I've been to a total stranger.

He's going to re-open the door with a gun pointing at your head, I muse.

But he drives off.

I collect my cash and dash back to the hotel.

I now have a clearer view of the salesman from earlier. He's pointing at watermelons on his fruit stall, and no doubt offering me a great bargain in a language I can't understand. The only umbrella anywhere in sight is clearly his own.

Chapter 11

Cover-Up City

Through the small city of Elazig my driver's car scoots as Turkish folk music blares from the vehicle's speakers.

A little more than one thousand kilometres southeast of Istanbul, Elazig is home to approximately three hundred thousand people. It almost cracks the list of Turkey's twenty most populous cities, and connects to Ankara and Istanbul through daily flights. Far less cosmopolitan than the latter, you won't be winning any arguments here with tourism officers about the existence of active church seats, Armenian or otherwise.

Its streets are narrower than Istanbul's, and though less populated, and certainly less of a touristic attraction, Elazig can at times feel more claustrophobic, denser, due to this lack of space. Honking repeatedly, my driver shows his displeasure when a police officer waves him to a stop to allow a large cluster of pedestrians passage.

On another occasion, the chauffeur confronts another car opposite him on the oncoming way when a narrow, uphill path will allow just one vehicle through at a time. For a moment, it looks like only a game of chicken will settle the dispute, until my driver, deflated, backs up and cedes the street.

Elazig grew out of a much smaller village, Mezre, at the foot of the hill where looms Kharpert (a name that combines a version of the Armenian word for rock, *kar*, and the Armenian word for fortress, *pert*), my ancestral home. My whole life the fortress-town's been practically mythological. Now at a pace of around forty kilometres an hour myth becomes reality, topped by a billowing Turkish flag.

Near as our written family records allow us to see, the Boudjikanians had made their home around Kharpert at least since the era of my grandfather's grandfather, Hagop Boudjikanian, who, unlike many of his descendants, seems to have been a burly, heavy-set man.

A bit of a bully and a difficult child, Hagop was known to terrorize other kids in the village. Growing up, family lore says, he turned his mercurial temperament and physicality toward defending his ethnic Armenian compatriots as tensions and unease grew between the former and the Turks. One legend has it he once drove off a gang of Kurds who had shut the water-well at Tchnkoush, the village near Kharpert where he lived as a young man, with only the help of a few friends.

His son, Hovhanness, grew up to become a philosophy professor at Euphrates College, an American-run institution. Named for the longest river in western Asia, which cascades from north of the city through to Syria and Iraq, the high school was first established as a seminary for American missionaries, before it opened up to the general population in 1878. For a short while, it was called Armenia College, but the discontent of Ottoman authorities prevailed, and the more innocuous name based on the body of water was adopted.

The actions of the Ottomans against the Armenians continued to grow in number and brutality, until they reached a climax in the early years of the twentieth century. Like a majority of Armenians, the Boudjikanians were then uprooted from their home once the deportations and genocide started in 1915.

There are now few Armenians living in Kharpert's modern-day descendant, Harput (a Turkified version of the Armenian name), or the bigger city we traverse at its base. Staff at the *Agos* paper told me they estimated about forty people in Elazig are of Armenian descent.

Good luck getting any of those to admit it, however. They either don't know or are too scared to speak of it publicly.

This has led to an amnesia about Armenians in the Elazig region. My ethnic Armenian guide, who acted as a translator throughout my stay in Turkey, would shrug off my concern whenever we spoke our native language within earshot of others. "They think we're speaking English," the guide would say.

Incidentally, I won't tell you the latter's name. I also won't disclose the identity of the one Elazig ethnic Armenian I convinced to grant me an interview, since they insisted on anonymity.

"There's my whole career here," the person says, proud of how far they've come, staying in their ancestral land. That candour, however, only goes so far. When I ask how they felt growing up with the knowledge the genocide occurred right at their doorstep, the person's careful not to mouth anything the least bit controversial.

"However you felt, I felt the same way too," the person says.

"As in, you were angry?" I pursue.

"However you felt, I felt the same way too," the person repeats.

"Hrant Dink spoke," the person snaps when I try to push for more. "What happened to him?"

Tough to argue with that.

*   *   *

Modern-day Elazig is a city of approximately three hundred thousand, near my ancestral home town of Kharpert. Staff at the Agos Turkish-Armenian newspaper tell me only about forty Armenians still live there.

Traces of denial, of silence, haunt Elazig and Kharpert if you know where to look. In the former, the three half-walls of what was once a Protestant church cast their shadow over a public parking lot. Such ruined Armenian churches are common throughout the country; many of those that were not destroyed in 1915 have either been converted to other uses or left to crumble into ruin.

It may have been the church where our family lore says Hagop converted from Apostolicism, also known as the Armenian Orthodox Church, the majority denomination for my people. This I will never know for sure, I tell myself, as I take pictures.

It must appear strange to the strangers around me; perhaps the beige brickwork and carved window-shapes in the walls mean nothing to them.

The remains of an old Armenian Protestant church in Elazig, in what has been converted into a parking lot.

Other seemingly innocuous places also mask brutal historical episodes. At a roughly half-hour drive from the city lies pristine Lake Hazar, surrounded by the equally picturesque Hazar Baba ("Thousand Fathers") mountains. The sky reflects so perfectly in Hazar's crystal-clear water you'd want to bathe eternally in its blue, then build yourself a chalet on the shore. It would be the type of place you would invite friends and family over to for summer or long-weekend getaways, with barbecues by day and marshmallows roasted on campfires by night.

Except, of course, if you happen to know your history; if you happen to know its waters were of a decidedly different hue in 1915.

That year, eyewitness testimony says, Turks threw Armenian corpses into Lake Hazar or buried them around the body of water.

Serene Lake Hazar near Elazig, where Turks threw thousands of Armenian corpses in 1915.

The American consul to the Kharpert region, Leslie Davis, toured the area and noted "hundreds of bodies and many bones" beneath the waves. Of the lake, he remarked "thousands and thousands of Armenians, mostly innocent and helpless women and children, were butchered on its shores and barbarously mutilated."

At Lake Hazar I watch waves lap the shore with morbid curiosity, flocks of airborne seagulls observing me overhead in turn. I muse about anything remaining down there nearly a century later.

Did they once take my great-grandfather Hovhanness away and deliver him, receding, into some other distant land? Or did he sink to the bottom of this lake? Was he killed and then dragged and dumped here? Or was he not among the thousands who wound up in these waters?

Just how did the mechanics of transporting all those bodies work? It took me and my guide a half-hour's bus ride out

The remains of a fortress wall in Kharpert, my ancestral home town in what is now eastern Turkey, and, below me, the modern city of Elazig.

of Elazig only to cover the distance here in the twenty-first century. It must have been a real pain to bring out the dead all the way from Kharpert in 1915. Far simpler, perhaps, to force the Armenians to walk to the lake, and kill them there.

It is entirely conceivable Davis may have passed by my great-grandfather's corpse, too, or that it was swallowed by the water's depths. My paternal grandfather, Hovhanness's son Armen, wrote of his dad's final fate and alluded to Kharpert's intellectual class being slaughtered near the lake.

Then there's Kharpert's walled fortress itself, outcroppings of dusty brown and grey brick walls jutting off a hill freckled with bushes. Unlike well-preserved Sultanahmet Square in Istanbul, there's barely a sense of any history here, barely a sense anyone cares to know what it used to be. Looking around me, it's easy to suppose I'm the only international traveller among

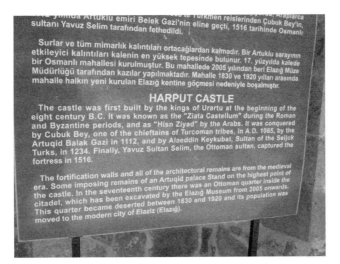

This sign omits mentioning my ancestors, or any Armenians, for that matter, ever lived in Kharpert (or, in Turkish, Harput). An example of how modern Turkey's genocide-denial policy extends to its tourism industry.

the small group of visitors wandering around, and I feel my guide and I are the only two people at all who have any idea what happened in Kharpert in 1915. Denial starts at the fortress gates. In white letters on a red backdrop, a bilingual English and Turkish sign explains these stones and this settlement were built by the Urartu Kingdom thousands of years ago.

It does not bother with the detail that the Armenian people descended from the Urartu. What it does say is that at the turn of the twentieth century "this quarter became deserted ... and its population was moved to the modern city of Elaziz (Elazig)."

This is the equivalent of a bad news conference, the unwilling subject impatiently yelling "no more questions" to reporters before rushing away from the microphone. "How many acts of genocide …" might a certain Reuters correspondent call to the ones who fashioned this banal bit of double-speak.

Around me other tourists, some Turks, leisurely walk around and pose for funny pictures, acting as one would at any sightseeing opportunity. I barely resist the urge to march up to them, and yell indignantly about what happened here ninety-seven years ago, how so much of what they are told by their political leaders on the subject is a lie.

Beneath me, golden fields scroll spectacularly to the horizon, the Hazar Baba summits above them floating like phantoms.

Who would up and leave this beautiful home for no reasons worthy of mention on signage destined for tourists?

Chapter 12

House and Home

It is May 17, 2012, and I'm sitting on a large rock in the walled ruins of Kharpert. Nearby is an example of what the Turkish Ministry of Culture and Tourism calls an Ottoman house. There isn't much to see now: a pile of grey-brown rocks almost flat against the ground, covered by a greenish tin roof.

The signage explains these houses were typically two storeys high, with couches surrounding a fireplace on the main-floor living room. A second storey would hold a summer living room, as well as the main bedroom.

Kharpert wasn't huge. It's not inconceivable someone sleeping in a second-storey bedroom could have woken up every morning to the sight of the three-thousand-year-old main castle tower topping the hill. I picture my grandfather doing this as a boy, gazing at the four dark arches by the sheer rockface underneath rolling white clouds. Did he do it a lot? Does one take such sights for granted when they are daily scenery?

Armen Boudjikanian would not speak of his youth to me or my siblings in Beirut. I remember him in his old age, of course, greeting us with candy and a smile in his apartment's

The four arches topping the remains of Kharpert's fortress.

high-ceilinged living room as soon as we stepped in through the cavernous entrance hallway. Sporting thick, curly white locks well into his late eighties (a feat neither his son nor grandsons will reproduce, I'm afraid), and wide, circular spectacles that lent him a somewhat owl-like air, he enjoyed telling us stories, just not those of his birthplace.

I hazily recall images of a much different man, quiet, brooding, hands clasped behind his back in the dark of night, walking silently through his home, likely assuming everyone else was asleep and therefore would not be watching him.

Were those his moments of recollection, glimpses through memory at a long-finished life in Kharpert, one violently taken and destroyed?

I can fill in some of the blanks, thanks to the writing he has left behind.

From there, we learn he was indeed excitedly staring out his window on that fateful day of May 1, 1915. Just as I have now waited, while shuttling between Elazig and the fortress-town, Armen was waiting for a hired carriage, one that was to take him, his dad, and the rest of their family down to Mezre. They had extended family there, including his father's brother, and were to go visit a newborn relative.

Instead, it was Turkish gendarmes who came knocking. They'd brought along a friend of Armen's dad, a poet named Tlgadintsi, who informed him the city's mayor wished to see them.

"One minute," Armen recalls his father responding before he hurriedly finished a shave. Then the strange cortege departed. Armen waited for his father to return and take them to Mezre.

When they came to drag Hovhanness out of his house that day, the Turkish gendarmes were under orders to get rid of the Armenian intellectual class first.

They did bring Hovhanness back home once more, at night, had him watch as they ransacked the place top to bottom. My grandfather recalls them going so far as to inspect the eggs under the family hen out in the courtyard, under suspicion the fragile shells could have been concealing some tiny bombs.

What they would have to fear from a philosophy professor, I cannot fathom.

Hovhanness was known for his intellectual defence of Armenian nationhood. In 1912, during a commemorative event folding in anniversaries of both the first Armenian-language book's publication (1512), and, somewhat belatedly, the invention of the Armenian alphabet itself (405 A.D.), he'd delivered a proud speech extolling the latter's virtues.

And so, when one gendarme, frustrated, questioned his colleagues, declaring, "It is obvious that there is no gun, bomb, or any other revolutionary object here, why are we wasting our time?" his superior officer responded, "His bomb is in his mind."

When they took Hovhanness away a second time from his home, the gendarmes also took bags full of his writings, books, and family portraits. "Don't be scared, he'll come back," they told the rest of the family, all smiles. He would never set foot in that house again.

Hovhanness would never be able to escape with his family, but in his prison cell he did see his son, my grandfather Armen, once. "[My father] … hugged me to his breast, started stroking my hair and kissing me," Armen, seven at the time, would later recall. "He was barely able to wear his usual smile, pretend to be happy, and issue a caring father's orders, telling me to behave, to not bother others in the house, to be kind, to take care of my sisters and brothers, to pray for him, so he might quickly return." That was the last time Armen saw him.

Days passed, during which, Armen maintained, all prisoners were tortured by the Turkish gendarmes guarding them.

"What gives you the right?" Hovhanness reportedly screamed in revolt, as his nails were pulled off and he was severely beaten.

"You were saying, 'Let's live as Armenians, let's die as Armenians,'" one of his jailors said, citing a passage of the professor's double-anniversary speech, "Well, now you live and die an Armenian. Your bomb is in this thick head of yours, I will make it explode."

When Armen's grandmother, Hovhanness's mother, went to see him next, she was denied. But a prison guard brandished Hovhanness's bloodied garments at her, telling her to take her son's clothes and wash them.

Pastor Ehmann, a German missionary who knew my family, smuggled them quietly down the hill to Mezre, hid them there in the home of Hovhanness's brother Mardiross.

Armen still refused to believe Hovhanness was gone for good, holding out hope his dad would return when the atrocities stopped, take them in a carriage back to Kharpert.

Instead, Turkish gendarmes caught up to the rest of the Boudjikanians and jailed them as well. If it weren't for another timely intervention by Ehmann, who managed to free them by personally pleading to connections he had among the military, they would have likely met the same fate as Hovhanness.

Ehmann was able to hide them for a few more years, until they left Kharpert for Beirut in 1922, avoiding the death marches that nearly annihilated my people.

* * *

Nowhere to be seen are the remains of Euphrates College where my great-grandfather Hovhanness taught psychology, philosophy, logic, morals, and social sciences. We know from old pictures it was situated somewhere on a hill, but you'd need more than that to find its location. The mount cleaving Kharpert above from Elazig below is mostly empty of ruins. At the bottom, one may glimpse remains of two structures, but I'm assured those are what's left of yet two more churches, not the school.

Portraits of Hovhanness show him in adulthood bearing a close resemblance to my father, the grandson he would never meet, though he sported a black moustache, a defining feature of male fashion in the Empire at the time.

Whereas in Kharpert I never have the chance to see where he used to work, I do stumble upon an old Euphrates College yearbook with his photo. To what would be the eternal amusement, I'm sure, of my colleagues in broadcasting and a whole legion of other people who have misspelled and/or mispro-nounced my name over the course of my life, the book dubs him "Hovhanness Buçigyan." Getting our family name wrong is at least a century-long endeavour, it would seem. Or, per-haps, Buçigyan did really exist, and the Ottoman Turkish gen-darmes' arresting my great-grandfather instead, and treating him as a dangerous revolutionary, was a serious case of mis-taken identity.

* * *

While Euphrates College has disappeared entirely, other build-ings representing Armenian culture have been repurposed or only partially destroyed. Hundred-year-old wooden doors guard the rooms of an ancient Armenian church now converted to somebody's home in Yavaş, a village to the north of Elazig. You may recognize the stone-carved Christian baptismal font in one corner if you look carefully enough, as my kindly guide tells me. But that, other than the shape of the building, is the last hint of what the structure once was.

Local lore has it that a century ago, an Armenian pastor and his family lived in the church themselves. The man of the cloth had a son, the type who makes friends easily. A girl living in the village, not of Armenian descent, caught his eye and they began chatting. It is said the father of the girl found out about her new male friend and was none too pleased.

You may believe he should have let the boy off with a warning. Perhaps the boy did something to merit harsher treat-ment. But the version of the tale I heard skips the details. It gets straight to the point: the father picked up his gun and shot the boy dead.

Lore says the father's rage did not end with the death of the boy who had befriended his daughter. He walked all the way to the boy's house, the Armenian church, and told the family they would all die unless they fled.

And so they ran away, leaving the temple in the hands of the father. He took it over, and it has never since been in the hands of an Armenian family.

*   *   *

To Elazig's southwest is another hidden sight, the ruins of a monastery known by the name of a village that surrounded it: Tadum. Unless you know something of Armenian architecture, you would be hard-pressed to see that those walls once held a church. There is no cross atop its beige summit, no traces of Armenian writing anywhere.

You'd be forgiven for assuming the whole area was never anything other than a children's playground. Some of them are kicking a white soccer ball around on the grassy turf as I arrive to take pictures. At least they've got goal-posts, and aren't using the monastery itself as a net.

A younger one among the kids is curious, wants to watch me at work. An elder leads him away. I continue snapping pictures in a dark chamber that was once a part of Tadum's monastery. I become dimly aware of some shouting outside. One voice I recognize as my guide's, the other as that of the chauffeur who drove us here. The third is definitely not the high-pitched squeal of any among the children who saw me earlier.

When I look, I see a man in the middle of a spirited dispute with my driver and translator.

Children kick a soccer ball around near the abandoned entrance of Tadum, a former Armenian monastery near Elazig.

More of the children playing soccer, shot through a window from inside Tadum.

The querulous fellow leaves them be and takes off before I reach the commotion. Assuming all is fine, I return to explore Tadum's desolate expanse.

I don't notice my driver is sitting back inside his car until he honks, clearly wanting my attention. He wants us to leave, and as I pack my belongings, my translator explains why. The man who came to yell at them now owns the land we've been stomping around.

We are not, apparently, the first Armenians to trespass on his property merely to gawk at some old rock, and he's tired of this. He insists he would let people freely do their sightseeing if they asked his permission first, but he will not tolerate intruders.

Besides, he's been taking good care of the old church, he says. Score.

* * *

Dead Armenians, too, are unwelcome in Elazig. Around three decades ago, Turkish authorities insisted the Armenian cemetery in the city had to go. It was too close to the centre, an ugly presence in the middle of booming infrastructure.

The few remaining Armenians who had any means at all agreed to move it. The cemetery is now near Khoulvenk, another village on the city's outskirts. Walled away from a surrounding field and accessible through a rust-coloured, metallic gate, it is one of the precious few places in the region where you can see crosses. That the crosses are mostly decorating tombstones is, I suppose, pretty much the point.

Khoulvenk has its own ruined monastery. A shepherd walks his flock near the grounds of the ruined structure when

The Armenian cemetery near Khoulvenk, a village in the Elazig area.

Grazing sheep walk past the ruined monastery of Khoulvenk. The structure may very well be what the village was named after, as the word appears to be a combination of the Armenian words *khoul* and *vank*, or *deaf* and *monastery*.

A brick with multiple crosses on the floor of the Khoulvenk monastery bears witness to what the building once was.

we arrive, but they don't wait. The wind carries the sheep's braying as they amble away from Khoulvenk, leaving pellets of dung behind.

There is a hollowed-out shape in the ground near the building: once a basin, I'm told, where it was believed bathing sick children would make them better. That'd be an unlikely cure now, filled as the basin is with dirt, discarded paper plates, plastic cups, and plastic bags.

Though smaller than the one at Tadum, the monastery here has slightly more circumstantial evidence of what it used to be: more crosses, etched into stones scattered on the floor between its four walls.

That other, infamous cross, the Nazis' swastika, is scratched in fading black on one of the walls. Maybe the artist who put it there was going for depth, making an allusion to Adolf Hitler's infamous quote when telling his officers about how they'd not be punished for the Holocaust: "Who, after all, speaks today of the annihilation of the Armenians?"

Or maybe they just figured swastikas were cool.

A wall with a decidedly different type of cross bears witness to the fact nothing is too sacred for graffiti.

Chapter 13

What to Do About the Past

Signs around Kharpert's walled fortress tell tourists not to stand for dirt or defacement of property. "If you see the castel [*sic*] being vandalised call gendareme on 156," they urge, referring visitors to a branch of the Turkish Armed Forces responsible for maintaining public order in areas outside police jurisdiction.

Funnily enough, some of the other signage at the site looks damaged, the red-and-white surface peeled back, revealing shiny grey metal beneath. And though the grounds are not particularly littered, you can still see discarded water bottles here and there.

A half-rebuilt wall, and some scaffolding hanging over a precipice, stand as testimony to the Turkish government's will to rebuild some of the fortress, at least, however else it may wish to continue to deny what actually transpired here ninety-seven years ago.

As I contemplate the place and record its sounds and sights, winds whistle into my microphone. I picture them carrying the voice of my great-grandfather, screaming all the way from a century ago, from wherever he went after he was killed.

He is asking me if I can forgive. The question catches me unawares. The rage consuming me since I first cast a glance at what happened to the Armenians here came as no surprise. You don't waltz into your ancestral homeland, ripped from your clan's hands, expecting to have a grand old time. But in my case at least, much less did I expect sudden reflections on pardon.

Maybe they should not have blindsided me so much. In Chad, I never asked the question to the survivors I met. People who remember watching their loved ones die before their eyes, who buried them with their bare hands, and who hoofed it on foot to refugee camps in another country, have other concerns than whether or not to forgive the genocidal regime that still does as it pleases in Khartoum.

But in Rwanda, "Do you forgive?" came up in almost every interview I conducted. With reconciliation the political order of the day, how could it not? And, unfailingly, every single one of the people I asked said they'd either already forgiven, or would if asked.

Rosette Sebasoni, who heard her five younger sisters scream for help from the bottom of a latrine until they could scream no more, said she'd forgive if asked.

If asked, though, is what's key here. I've never been asked. The Armenians have never been asked. My great-grandfather, for reasons that require no explaining, will never be asked.

At best, we've been given false equivalences about how Turks died, too, as "it was war time." Heck, in 2005, I interviewed the Turkish consul in London, England, for a university project on conflict in communities. Between taking sips of his Turkish coffee (paranoid me refused a cup, of course, settling for a glass of water) with the jolly grin of a cheerful host, he told me both people enjoy kebab, after all, so why can't everyone just get along?

At worst, we've been accused of conducting genocide ourselves, a difficult claim to support for anyone with a basic sense of demographics.

So, given all this, what does one do? Successive Turkish governments know recognition will bring with it financial and land claims, a large part of why they continue to deny. Yet, on the other hand, as striking as historic Armenia's landscapes are, I have a hard time picturing whole communities of diaspora Armenians deciding overnight to return to their old homeland, if, miraculously, some form of settlement were achieved. Most of us now won't move to the current existing country of Armenia, after all.

It's not that diaspora Armenians do not have any attachment to the small, mountainous state. It's that, like me, a great many are descendants of Armenians who lived in eastern Turkey before the genocide. It was that land, those people, the Ottoman Empire controlled. It was for those Armenians a final solution was devised. What is now Armenia proper was out of the Turks' immediate grasp. The Armenians living within the Empire's borders, though, could not be *easily* disposed of or forgotten. They did not wish to blend and become one with the Turkish population; they spoke a different language and prayed from a different holy book.

By 1915, Armenians were one of the few large Christian populations left within the crumbling Ottoman Empire, and for the Young Turks' ethnically pan-Turkic dream country, that just wouldn't do. There is some grim irony to the fact Armenians officially accepted Christianity as a national religion in the year 301 A.D., the same three digits that comprise the name of that article in the Turkish penal code that makes speaking about the genocide an illegal act.

All this knowledge of this dark history defines the prism through which diaspora Armenians perceive Armenia itself, too. Like many, I've made that trip, and like many, one of the first sights I'd wanted to see was not actually in Armenia, but Turkey.

Right on the border between the two, it loomed purple and hazy out of ancient history: the two summits of Mount Ararat, the biblical resting place of Noah's Ark, an eternal symbol of what Armenians have lost, of the chasm between them and the Turks.

In a region that is covered in so many mountain ranges locals would be hard-pressed to name them all, Ararat towers above most. Lesser Ararat, or Pokr Massis, as Armenians call it, already looms high at 3,896 metres. Its big brother, Greater Ararat or Medz Massis, shoots up further, to 5,137 metres. This does not quite place it on the list of the world's highest peaks, but it does make the dormant volcano an attractive proposition for alpinists who want to start smaller before tackling the likes of Everest.

There is perhaps no other country in the world that attaches so much importance to a geographical feature that actually remains outside its borders. In Armenia, you can buy beer, wine, and brandy named after the mountain (and, naturally, an alternate brandy named after Noah), or visit a large field in its shadow, also bearing its name. You can spend days trying to figure out the best vantage point to see the two peaks, hoping the fog will dissipate just enough for a nice view. And when that does happen, you can spend untold hours and data trying to capture their majesty in pictures, or, after a while, give up just to stare at them. If you're unfortunate enough not to receive one clear day to glimpse Ararat, you can always buy one of the million Ararat souvenir posters, magnets, or key chains, or go catch a soccer game featuring the national team named after the two summits. You can eat at an Ararat restaurant, book a party at an Ararat reception hall, or stay at an Ararat hotel.

Some diaspora Armenians actively look out the airplane window as the craft prepares to land in Yerevan, hoping for a top view. Local Armenians are so used to the sight it becomes a thermometer for them. "Pokr Massis is naked," one might be heard saying on a particularly hot summer's day, meaning the small peak's snowy cap has melted off completely. Armenian airport authorities stamp your passport with an illustration of the omnipresent silhouettes along with your single-entry visa when you arrive, and, of course, they have also appeared on Armenian currency. They are the central feature of the country's coat of arms. All this does not begin to explore how prominent the mountain is in the diaspora, too. Remember Soghomon Tehlirian, who had killed Talaat Pasha, one of the genocide's main architects? Well, Tehlirian is buried in a cemetery named after Ararat in Fresno, California. Small wonder filmmaker Atom Egoyan named his genocide epic *Ararat* in 2002. Little else would have sufficed.

The mountain's iconography, always present both literally and figuratively, leaves these questions about the past and forgiveness lingering on the minds of Armenians. Ararat is a beautiful, forbidding sight for anybody who visits Armenia. But for the descendants of the survivors, it is more. It serves as an everlasting reminder: Do not forget what evil befell your forefathers here beneath my skirts all those years ago.

What does one do?

On one of my visits to Kharpert, I hear people who are clearly not Turkish. They speak English, which I've barely heard since landing in Turkey, and certainly nowhere in the Elazig region. One asks another for a reminder of a certain nickname for the area surrounding the fortress-town. "The Golden What of Kharpert do they call this place?"

"Vosgetashd, that Armenian word for Golden Valley," her friend responds. You don't use that word unless you're Armenian.

I insinuate myself into their conversation by offering to take a picture of the two of them, but they refuse. Maybe they're as paranoid and suspicious as I've been lately, seeing spies everywhere. "Are you Armenian?" I ask, and they confess. I tell them I'm an Armenian from Montreal myself, and soon I find out they're part of an organized group touring the entirety of historic Armenia, not just Kharpert.

To these pilgrims, too, I do not bring up forgiveness. Granted, it would have been a weird subject to raise out of the blue with people you've known for all of five minutes, but I suspect length of time does not have as much to do with it as the expectation that I can predict their answers.

For diaspora Armenians, these issues are never forgotten, true, but they tend to ebb and flow in importance according to the time of year. Around April 24, every year, it seems the thoughts will never quite go away. During visits to Armenia and Turkey, they rise, pointedly demanding attention.

But for the Armenians who live in Turkey, these questions preoccupy in a much more concrete way, much more permanently. *Agos* staff say that since Hrant Dink's death in 2007, the remembrance day of his killing attracts thousands of protestors annually. That would have been unthinkable about a decade ago, when mention of the Armenian Question barely ever surfaced in Turkish media.

The Armenian I interviewed in Elazig, who is too fearful for their life to agree to be named, is conflicted about recognition and forgiveness. "It would be good," I succeed in making them concede, if the government acknowledged the genocide.

They remember being around fifteen years old when they first heard of the massacre from their grandfather, a survivor. The latter said Turks wiped out nearly his entire clan, fifty-five people, a whole neighbourhood.

But the politics of recognition, and their consequences on the lives of Turkish Armenians, have tempered their enthusiasm for justice. "We don't get mixed up in diaspora talks," as the Elazig Armenian sums up, "we suffer the results."

And when it's more than just talk, the results can be worse. Excessive zeal for justice led Armenians down dark paths a few decades ago. In the '70s and '80s, the now-disbanded ASALA (Armenian Secret Army for the Liberation of Armenia) and Justice Commandos of the Armenian genocide (JCAG) groups, classified as terrorist organizations by the United States, staged a number of paramilitary operations to pressure Turkey into recognizing the genocide. Nearly fifty diplomats were killed, all told, and civilians died, too.

My Armenian interviewee recalls being a guest at a fancy dinner in Elazig when the televised broadcast of one such act came on. As other attendees began seeing the imagery, our Elazig Armenian was the recipient of an increasingly cold reception.

"Instead of staying two hours, I stayed fifteen minutes," they say, and they left, worried about their safety.

All of which, of course, fails to answer the basic question: Do I forgive?

No.

I'd like the answer to be yes. I sense my great-grandfather would want it to be yes, as well. It does feel like the type of choice one would be expected to make a century later, letting bygones be bygones and burying the hatchet and all.

But that option, forgiveness, can only be weighed once I'm asked.

Epilogue

Origins and Returns

In Istanbul's airport at the crack of dawn I struggle to stay awake, firmly clutching my suitcase and my carry-on while taking in the first signs of activity as airline booths slowly swirl to life … there to Libya, there, to Uzbekistan. Before this trip, Uzbekistan was not somewhere, some real place, I could get to by hopping on a relatively short flight. It was somewhere James Bond might have checked out in an action-packed pre-credits sequence in one of his movies.

I pass the time by texting and emailing friends and family to remind them I'll be home shortly. There are few replies, as the sun isn't exactly up halfway across the world. One friend answers, explains she and her husband have just been to Newfoundland, and boasts about the beauty of St. John's, right on the ocean. Another piece of Canadiana I've never experienced, I tell myself, since I spend the majority of my travel time and budget on overseas adventures.

Soon enough, I begin to hear a smattering of that easily identifiable Quebec French dialect, Joual, and spot a handful of passengers sitting across from me who must also be headed to Paris and then back home to Montreal. Unlike me, they all appear to be of French descent.

So it's not difficult to extrapolate a conversation with one of them would inevitably lead to their asking me that perpetual "Where are you from?" question. And I'm more confused than ever about answering it.

I should be able to say "from here." I've just flown a little more than an hour from the area of Turkey my ancestors called home for untold generations, after all.

But that can't be right, can it?

You don't pack your luggage full of souvenir key chains depicting an iconic piece of architecture from the place you've been for your family "back home" if "home" is actually "here." You do that with the Eiffel Tower or the Statue of Liberty, not with Kharpert's Fortress.

And yet they're there, little off-white trinkets, that Turkified name Harput etched at their base, next to the handful of multi-coloured pebbles from Kharpert I stuffed in a glass jar, next to the fridge-magnet pictures of the same structure.

How can Kharpert be home when my mother tongue remains so obscure and so unfamiliar locals who hear it are just as likely to assume I'm speaking English?

Where are you from?

No matter the tension the Armenians from Istanbul and the handful from Kharpert feel, they would never have trouble answering this question. I see their point now, when they ask why they should ever be made to move, when they say this is their home and they've been here forever.

So, where am I from?

It's not the modern country of Armenia, where we have family but cannot say the majority of our clan has ever lived. I was not born there, have visited it, and have certainly felt a vivid kinship with the people, the culture and history … but you won't find traces of Boudjikanians there reaching very far back.

"So, where, then?" My imaginary interlocutor still prods.

The annoyance is perhaps infinitesimally close to what the displaced Darfuri refugees living in Chad must experience on a daily basis.

It's not quite Canada, though that's where I've grown up and lived most of my life. Of course, whether anyone can legitimately lay claim to being "from" a country of immigrants besides the First Nations is the subject of books more voluminous than this one.

Besides, let's face it, the majority of people I've known during the entire first half of my life are ethnically Armenian, thanks to my attendance at a diaspora grade/high school. The effect was rather jarring once I hit higher education studies. In the first two years after high school, which, for most Quebec students, take place at a CEGEP (Collège d'éducation générale et professionelle, or, in English, a professional and general education college), a type of intermediary step between senior high and university, I'd mostly kept to a social circle of Armenian friends. Many of them had finished high school with me. Sure, having them in exactly the same classes was a rarity, but a group of us would inevitably find some spot to gather between lectures, typically around a cafeteria lunch table. Occasionally, we'd try seeing if we could fit into the same schedule when it came to general education courses.

One day, in a history of literature class where I had none of my lifelong friends as classmates, our teacher looked at the roomful of thirty-something students and asked if anyone in attendance knew enough about their family history to name at least one of their great-great grandparents. True to that bizarre meaning of my first name, my hand shot up like a lightning bolt, and I expected the same from a majority of the other students.

My teacher swiveled his neck left to right, scanning the width of the lecture hall, his thin-rimmed glasses framing a sad but hardly surprised look. When I saw his expression, I glanced behind my shoulder myself, and saw, very surprised, only one other hand raised up. It was that of an Asian student seated far in the back.

"See? Only two people," the teacher said with some disappointment. He asked us each our ethnic backgrounds. To this day I'm sure everyone recognized the word *Japanese*, but unsure many people in the class reacted to *Armenian*. If my teacher had never heard of it, he was too graceful to say. "Two people that are known for remembering their past," he instead explained to those around him. "So who can you name?" he asked me.

"Hagop, my grandfather's grandfather," I answered, for which I earned a somewhat quizzical look. "It's the Armenian form of Jacob," I elaborated, receiving a nod of recognition. With the hushed murmurs around me, any urge I may have had to go on and deliver The Lecture died right there in my mouth. After class, I related my disbelief about the whole episode to Armenian friends around the cafeteria table.

"So, where?" My fictitious airport interviewer would still, no doubt, persist, after hearing this anecdote. As revealing as it may be about my family history, it doesn't quite answer their question, after all.

I was born in Beirut.

"Ah, Lebanese, then. You're Arab."

Yes and no. Not Arab.

"But you're from Lebanon."

Yes, but then, lots of Armenians are. At one point, Lebanon held the largest population of Armenians on the planet outside of Armenia.

"But then, aren't Armenians Arab?" (And though this particular situation is hypothetical, I've been asked the question many a time).

No, following 1915, a majority of them were only there because … which brings us back to historic Armenia, and, well, The Lecture.

These are admittedly inconsequential ruminations. Next to the fact that, following the Armenian genocide, the world has gone on to repeatedly fail persecuted communities facing destruction, from Ukrainians and Jews to Cambodians, Rwandans, Bosnians, and Darfuris, it doesn't matter that I don't really have an answer to the made-up query.

And yet, there's the nagging notion, which can't be all that different from Faridah Badawi's longing to one day return to Darfur: Why shouldn't I be able to say "from here" and just leave it at that?

In some future world, where justice is never restored for the Darfuris, where the displaced can never go home because neither current Sudanese president Omar al-Bashir nor any of his successors are ever held to account for the crimes against humanity in Sudan, these parallels transcend the superficial.

In this future world, Badawi's children are born in the single-room Farchana "maternity ward," and raised amidst the camp's overcrowded classrooms and trade workshops. They may forever straddle the border between the tents and straw huts of the refugee camps in their adopted home country of Chad and faraway, mythical Zaghawa in Darfur, attempting to figure out if they are walking by their grandfather's unmarked grave near the ruins of the Arba Mouli public market.

These children, too, are marked by the stories of what they've heard happen to their ancestors. They, too, want apologies and justice.

Genocide is not only whom and what it destroys; it is also whom and what it leaves behind.

That can be a century of denial and neglect; or two decades of uneasy reconciliation; or one decade of continued suffering as perpetrators sit atop their thrones unpunished.

That denial can seep so deep the victims themselves may start to get in on the act. In Turkey, some of the taboos had been around before the crime itself. Recall the name change of the school where my great-grandfather taught, from Armenia College to Euphrates. Fast-forward a century; look at how a generation of survivors, including my grandfather, did not wish to discuss with their descendants what they'd been through, how they rebuilt their lives from scratch in a strange new land; the struggle I felt trying to convince my anonymous ethnic Armenian interviewee to open up about the genocide in Elazig, and how I had no comeback when they reminded me of Hrant Dink's dark fate. Now, look at how I myself clammed up about my Armenian identity, which I'm happy to go on about whenever someone shows the least amount of curiosity, when asked where I'm from, twice, by the ostensibly random stranger in Istanbul at night.

In Rwanda, schoolchildren are asked to speak up about their identities, but are taught they are all Rwandan, encouraged to forget the Tutsi and Hutu epithets. This is deemed necessary for future stability, but it can't be particularly pleasant for some survivors. One, after all, told me they rather resented the "Rwandan genocide" label, and insisted it should be called the "Tutsi genocide," because that was the specific, targeted ethnic identity of the vast majority of victims.

For Armenians and Rwandans, the immediate, physical violence has passed. Psychological wounds scar the collective psyche of both people. For Darfuris, both types are still there. Those who have survived the brutal killings endure only in great hardship, questioning how the world has passed them by with no sustained, demonstrable care for their plight.

Genocide is also the inaction of the international community.

"I am confident," Henry Morgenthau, Sr., U.S. Ambassador to the Ottoman Empire, wrote of the Armenian genocide in his memoirs published in 1919, "that the whole history of the human race contains no such horrible episode as this." How did he react, one wonders, to the news of the Jewish Holocaust in his last years, an atrocity stopped only after six million lost their lives during the next World War?

"It is important that the world know that these killings were not spontaneous or accidental," President Bill Clinton said on March 25, 1998, during a visit to Rwanda. "The international community," he added to applause, "together with nations in Africa, must bear its share of responsibility for this tragedy as well. He continued, "We did not act quickly enough after the killing began ... We did not immediately call these crimes by their rightful name: genocide ... We owe to those who died and those who survived who loved them, our every effort to increase our vigilance and strengthen our stand against those who would commit such atrocities in the future here or elsewhere."

That was fewer than four years after the Rwandan genocide. It's been more than twice as long since Darfur started. Though then U.S. Secretary of State Colin L. Powell did call the events there "genocide" in 2004 from the safety of American soil, no sitting member of any Western government has gone to Darfur to speak the same kind of truth to power.

Indeed, it is unclear any will by the time Badawi's hypothetical children are old enough to visit their homeland.

Has there been any progress since 1915? There is the fact we have an International Criminal Court now, the body that indicted Bashir on war crimes charges. Of course, nobody has actually made good on booking him, but at least the warrant exists.

It's several steps beyond the judicial mechanisms around at the dawn of the twentieth century.

In fact, Polish juror Raphael Lemkin would not actually coin the term *genocide* to describe the Holocaust until he turned back to examine the Armenian massacres of 1915 themselves.

So, what good could come of it for the Badawi children and their kin?

Some … if the arrest is ever upgraded from theory to reality, and if there are trials, and if there is a verdict, and if there is a change in government, and if there is a will to provide restitution to the Darfuri survivors. Then, maybe, Badawi's children would be able to say, without eternal soul-searching, where they're from.

Of course, there are more "ifs" in that last paragraph than in any other in this book.

But our evolution as an ethically-minded species will depend on how unconditionally we stand up to injustice across the world everywhere, refusing to draw the line at political or economic interest.

We're admittedly closer to that point now than one hundred years ago, but still not quite there.

Some argue international intervention is not the way to go, for a litany of reasons. Motivations of the intervening powers will never be pure enough, they say; or meddling only exacerbates existing tensions; or, worse, some combination of those factors.

All this could very well be true. But ask any descendants of those on the receiving end of the machete, or bullet, or stuck inside the gas chamber: the protests are usually not about the international community interfering too much.

What hope for justice is there, if any, if the world casts its eyes away? A long, slow, torturous one. Though the vast majority of serious academics and historians has long abandoned the idea of a debate about history, and calls the Armenian genocide exactly that, it has taken decades of international pressure and lobbying for Armenians to convince the governments of about thirty countries to do the same. For various geopolitical reasons, some of the bigger fish out there, such as the United States of America or the United Kingdom, have yet to do so, though politicians sure enjoy trotting out such promises during election time.

Of course, the key country in all of this is Turkey. In the past decade, the genocide there has become genuine fodder for academic and public discussion.

More progressive Turkish academics and media have gone on the record stating the Armenian genocide as fact, or at least insisted on vigorous debate over the issue, criticizing the government's refusal to face its bloody past. Some of them have actually done it without facing legal repercussions.

Though clinging to its denialist agenda, Ankara has made some very gradual concessions to its Armenian minority. It allowed the restoration of one ancient Armenian church, Sourp Khatch ("Holy Cross," in Armenian), on Aghtamar or Akhtamar Island, in the middle of Lake Van, though the structure serves not as a place of worship but a museum, and has not just a cross mounted atop its roof, but a Turkish flag.

There's been Abdullah Demirbas, the Kurdish mayor of a central district in the town of Diyarbakir, eastern Anatolia, admitting his ancestors visited unspeakable acts upon Armenians.

There's the touristic Istanbul map actually recognizing the existence of an Armenian Patriarchate, though it may take a bit of a raised voice with the staffer at the tourist office to admit the place exists before he'll start pointing at it.

And the changing attitudes sometimes extend to those on the other side of this argument. I'm still not ready to forgive for what happened to my great-grandfather, but can now see a world where I'm able to do so if an apology is ever made.

This may seem insignificant, but consider where I was at the beginning of this trip: expecting Turkey to be the most difficult leg of the journey, and it was. But, unlike what I anticipated in my worst nightmares, I was not handcuffed and carted off to prison as soon as I set foot inside the airport. Officially, I was not so much as interrogated a single time while I was in the country. Of course, I say this knowing it has one of the worst rates for imprisoned journalists anywhere in the world, so I may just have gotten very lucky. But still ....

Never would I have foretold the number of times a total stranger would stop me and my guide on the street and invite us for a glass of *chai* in front of their home or in an alley. It's a Turkish tradition to sit on small wooden stools barely rising above the ground and consume the dark tea in glasses that fit in the palm of your hand, sometimes spending hours in idle conversation. Of course, we were ever cautious, and I do not recall revealing the purpose of my trip to any of those welcoming us for a chat, least of all to a man who said he was a police officer in the small town of Sivis near Hazar Lake (was that some sort of unofficial interrogation?), but still ....

One of my last meals with my guide in Elazig was inside a small food truck serving durums, a type of doner-like sandwich that comes double-wrapped in pita. I'm fully aware of the irony in writing a paragraph about changing attitudes in Turkey as I omit the identity of my guide for fear of putting them in danger, but still … indulge me.

It was a quiet, inelegant meal, in a quiet, inelegant place. A fly or two buzzing around in the improperly aerated vehicle's oven-warm heat, for good measure. We got a couple of *tahn* (yogourt-based) drinks from the man who served us, too. He opened up my friend's can immediately as he gave them their food. He gave me my can unopened. The paranoid Armenian in me immediately suspected ill treatment, once more. My guide, perhaps surmising my mistrust, pointed out he only did that because my food wasn't ready yet.

I'd like to hope ill treatment won't be my first hunch on my next visit.

And, maybe, if I'm lucky, there will be no more denial Armenians actually ever lived in the old fortress-town of Kharpert. I'm not expecting the Turkish flag atop it to be taken down anytime soon. After all, despite official acknowledgement Aghtamar was an Armenian building, the church remains decorated with the red-and-white moon and star.

Perhaps, though, the signage saying Kharpert's mysterious, unidentified inhabitants just left the premises, with no explanation provided, will be slightly modified. Perhaps the repairs on the fortress will be completed, and there will be some acknowledgement the ruins at the bottom of the hill used to be churches.

Perhaps, by then, locals will have heard enough about Armenians they will not suppose it is English when they hear my native language. Perhaps I will be able to go interview my anonymous Elazig Armenian without their fearing for their lives, or voyage far enough east in Turkey to walk up close to Ararat, to see it from the other side of the border. Perhaps the demonstrations commemorating Hrant Dink's death will swell beyond the streets of Istanbul. Perhaps the protests will swell beyond Hrant Dink's death, remembering the Armenian genocide as loudly as it is remembered elsewhere in the world. Perhaps Law 301 will be repealed, and commentators at *Agos* and other brave publications will not have to fear prosecution or worse anytime they write the G word. Perhaps Turkey will no longer welcome Sudanese president Omar al-Bashir with open arms despite the arrest warrants the latter has been issued (look it up — Ankara is hardly alone in this but it did happen). Perhaps I will not be stopped in Istanbul in the evening and asked uncomfortable questions by a well dressed man behind the wheel of a nice car, who may or may not be a spy.

Perhaps I won't have to think twice about the contents of every email I send to friends and family while I'm in the country. Perhaps they won't be afraid something could go horribly wrong during the visit. Perhaps it will be possible to openly interview government officials without having to mince my words. Perhaps I won't be too shy to tell other Kharpert visitors the actual history of what happened there. Perhaps it will be easier for them to stomach since they will already have heard so much more by then.

Perhaps Turkey will stop protesting and pulling its ambassador to Ankara every time another country's legislature adopts language calling the 1915 events a genocide. Perhaps its own government will focus on accepting this historical truth instead of pumping cash into a well-oiled denial campaign as tired as it is tiring for Armenians. Perhaps Turkish leaders will not be able to keep convincing their own citizens who dig up secret connections to the Armenian genocide in their own personal family histories that they do not have a real grasp on what happened. Perhaps the leaders will come to accept there is no more need for a joint historical commission to look into the events, since most historians have said there is no ambiguity to the veracity and intent of the massacres.

And maybe, just, maybe, answering where I'm from will be a slightly less awkward proposition by then.

Afterword

On a warm day in July 2016, I stood at the podium where Adolf Hitler addressed some of his largest rallies, in Nuremberg, on Zeppelin Field.

Picturing the vast, bare space beneath me filled with thousands of followers applauding the genocidal madman's words, it was not much of a leap to see how power could have gone to Hitler's head, and how he and his supporters fed off each other's energy in the lead-up to the horrors of the Second World War.

Of course, there is more you can do in Nuremberg than see Hitler's stomping grounds. You can visit its Palace of Justice and you can walk inside Courtroom 600, where the Nazis were tried for their crimes.

You can lay down your backpack, arm your camera, and make like any of the other tourists taking in the sights. Idle on the benches where the audience sat during those historic proceedings, march right up to the justices' seats.

I was in Germany by happenstance on a European vacation, not intending to work on the book at all. I remember finding it remarkable how sharp a contrast this inadvertent addition to my "journey through genocide" made with my experience in Turkey in 2012.

There, I'd had to resist an urge to yell out loud about the fabrications on the tourism signs the Turkish government had installed around my ancestral hometown of Kharpert, all in a bid to cover up the fact that Armenians were massacred during the genocide.

In Germany, the government welcomed you to explore the history of how Nazi war criminals were prosecuted and convicted.

And whereas I'd ended my earlier trip with the cautious optimism reflected in the epilogue, by 2016 it had considerably dwindled. If anything, Turkey has edged further away from owning up to its responsibility for the Armenian genocide.

Meanwhile, the rise of ISIS in the Middle East and the violent birth of South Sudan, splintering from Omar al-Bashir's government in Khartoum, have both deepened the respective refugee crises in those regions and set the stage for more crimes against humanity, with the perpetrators largely unpunished.

The continued lack of any true sanctions for al-Bashir's actions in Darfur has bred more permissiveness in the international community about the mass, indiscriminate slaughter of civilians.

In Syria, an increasingly volatile situation has sent refugees of all ethnic and political stripes fleeing what used to be one of the more stable countries in the Middle East.

In 2015, I was among many journalists in Western countries assigned to cover the arrival of Syrians landing at airport terminals or settling into their new apartments.

On one such occasion I was dispatched to Pierre Elliott Trudeau International near Montreal to interview passengers stepping off a plane and uniting with their sponsors or loved ones.

Among those waiting at international arrivals, I met two teenage Syrian-Armenian brothers, Sarkis and Keyork Keyork.

They had managed to land in Canada before their parents, and were now anxiously awaiting them. The four had been separated for about a year, paperwork from a temporary refugee camp in Lebanon taking longer to process for husband and wife than it had for their two sons.

The two boys said a few words for my camera, but were likely too overcome with emotion at the idea of their impending reunion to say much more, or perhaps they were a little shy.

At any rate, the tearful embrace did occur when the Keyorks' parents showed up. As I watched it unfold, I envisaged a long view of that family's history. If they all lived in Syria, it is likely some of their ancestors escaped from the genocide in 1915.

Now, one hundred years later, here they were again, escaping.

Despite all the difficulties that lay ahead for them, I was also aware of how much luckier they were than a lot of others displaced by war, those stuck on crummy lifeboats; in overcrowded camps; or, worse, simply killed.

As the situation in Syria has worsened, all sides in the conflict have been to blame for at least some civilian deaths, if not outright crimes against humanity.

It has been years since the U.N. has drawn up a list of potential suspects for future prosecution at the International Criminal Court. The document, though confidential for now, reportedly includes names from both rebel groups and the government.

Over in South Sudan, the finger-pointing seems more one-sided, with an ironically similar modus operandi to that of the government it broke away from in 2011: namely, carry out attacks on ethnic tribes and later blame some faceless rebel groups for all the trouble.

The testimonies of those who have fled South Sudan indeed frighteningly echo those of the Darfuri refugees I interviewed in Chad — peaceful village lives disrupted, family members killed, homes set ablaze, a mad rush to escape with one's life.

Yet another crisis looms in Myanmar.

There, the U.N. says a Muslim minority population in northern Rakhine State, near Bangladesh, endures death and suffering as many attempt escaping to the latter country.

Here, again, the language used by interviewees to describe their ordeal uncomfortably resembles a lot of stories from my travels. In one passage, a U.N. report mentions intellectual and religious leaders getting rounded up and taken away first … which is almost lifted from the playbook of how Ottoman gendarmes treated Armenians in 1915.

That same report features testimony from more than 220 refugees who now live across the border in Bangladesh. One woman describes trying to hide in her father's house, only for soldiers to force them to leave the structure as they set fire to it, and the man burning to death inside.

The interviewees have cited men wearing Myanmar army or police uniforms behind the killings, using military ordnance. This, while the government restricts journalists from accessing the area.

Syria, South Sudan, Myanmar. These are but three crises among many the world over. Counting them all may lead one to despair over ever seeing justice done.

And, long after these terrible events have been tended to, societies where they occurred will still grapple with their dark legacies.

When I stopped over in Germany, I also visited Bayreuth, a small town in Bavaria that continues to host an annual Richard Wagner festival, which is sold out every summer. Set inside an ornate building called the Wagner Festspielhaus, itself located in an idyllic park, the event admits Wagner's ties to the Nazis.

Wander among the perfectly manicured lawns, colourful beds of flowers, and trimmed bushes of the park, and you will happen upon shrines to musicians who used to have prominent careers with this festival until they were told it had to be otherwise. Here, learn about Arnold Rosé, a violinist and concert master who "played in Bayreuth from 1889 to1896, there accused of being a 'Jew.'" There, learn of Hans Venus, himself called a "quarter Jew." Then there is a Ferdinand Mehl, deemed "politically unacceptable" because of his membership in a communist party.

It is certainly more than a little awkward to discover these memorials in the middle of the gorgeous, peaceful gardens that form the backdrop to the Wagner concerts, but, again, Germany's acknowledgement of and repentance for the Holocaust mean one can at least have this kind of honest confrontation with history.

One can only wish and hope this will one day be possible for the two Sudans, Syria, Myanmar, and Turkey.

Acknowledgements

I would like to offer my sincere gratitude to all genocide survivors who decided to share their stories of trauma and terror for the journalism behind this book. It is one thing to live through some of the horrors these people have seen, and another to experience them all over again in memory during interviews.

My thanks as well to journalist colleagues, writers, academics, and other experts who provided insight and paved the way for my travels by illuminating me with their own experiences, helping to navigate bureaucracy, and in some cases taking much-needed critical glances at very unpolished manuscript drafts: Peter Johnson, Melissa Kent, Loreen Pindera, David Gutnick at CBC among others, Nicholas Kristof, Graeme Smith, Kyle Matthews, Gary Geddes, Mark Abley, Hourig Attarian, the staff at the United Nations High Commission for Refugees (UNHCR) in Chad, and many others I am certain I forget, to my shame.

I will always be grateful to Dundurn Press for picking up the book, believing in its importance, and seeing it through to publication. A particular shout-out to my thoughtful editor Dominic Farrell, for going through it with such a keen, careful eye and improving it immensely with his suggestions.

This project would have been impossible without the moral support of loved ones who encouraged me to make the trip, pushed me to write the book afterwards, and in many cases also read its early versions: my amazing parents, Adom and Aida Boudjikanian, who must have sifted through more drafts than anyone should have to; my siblings, Armen and Lory, and their spouses Taline and Hovig; my aunt Ani Boudjikanian; my friends Haig Toutikian, Alex Leduc; and many others.

Bibliography

BOOKS

Akçam, Taner. *A Shameful Act: The Armenian Genocide and the Question of Turkish Responsibility*. New York: Picador, 2007.

Balakian, Grigoris. *Armenian Golgotha: A Memoir of the Armenian Genocide, 1915–1918*. Translated by Peter Balakian and Aris Sevag. New York: Alfred A. Knopf, 2009.

Boudjikanian, Armen. "His Bomb Is In His Mind." In *The Boudjikanian Clan's Story*, 6–10. Beirut: G. Doniguian and Son Printing House, 1974. In Armenian.

Davis, Leslie A. *The Slaughterhouse Province: An American Diplomat's Report on the Armenian Genocide, 1915–1917*. *2nd ed.* New Rochelle: Aristide D. Karatzas, Publisher, 1990.

Gourevitch, Philip. *We Wish to Inform You That Tomorrow We Will Be Killed with Our Families: Stories from Rwanda*. New York: Picador,1998.

Grzyb, Amanda, ed. *The World and Darfur: International Response to Crimes Against Humanity in Western Sudan*. Montreal: McGill-Queen's University Press, 2009.

Hamilton, Rebecca. *Fighting for Darfur: Public Action and the Struggle to Stop Genocide.* New York: Palgrave Macmillan, 2011.

Kevorkian, Raymond. *Le Génocide des Arméniens.* Paris: Odile Jacob, 2006. In French.

Lochner, Louis P. *What About Germany?* New York: Dodd, Mead & Co.,1942.

Lonely Planet. *Africa.* 12th ed. Victoria: Lonely Planet, 2010.

Lonely Planet. *Turkey.* 12th ed. London: Lonely Planet, 2011.

Melvern, Linda. *Conspiracy to Murder: The Rwandan Genocide.* London: Verso, 2004.

Morgenthau, Henry. *Ambassador Morgenthau's Story.* New York: Doubleday, Page & Co., 1919.

ELECTRONIC MEDIA

Arsu, Sebnem, and Susanne Fowler. "Armenian-Turkish Unity at Slain Editor's Funeral." *New York Times.* January 24, 2007, www.nytimes.com/2007/01/24/world/europe/24turkey. html?_r=0.

Borg, Yesim, and Tracy Wilkinson. "Journalist Slain in Turkey." *Los Angeles Times.* January 20, 2007, http:// articles.latimes.com/2007/jan/20/world/fg-journalist20.

"Canadian Parliament Recognizes Armenian Genocide." *CBC News.* April 25, 2004, cbc.ca/news/canada/canadian-parliament-recognizes-armenian-genocide-1.509866.

"Chad Profile — Timeline." *BBC News.* March 27, 2015, bbc. com/news/world-africa-13164690.

Charbonneau, Louis. "Syria Government, IS Commit Crimes Against Humanity: UN-backed Inquiry." *Reuters.*

February 22, 2016, www.reuters.com/article/us-mideast-crisis-syria-un-idUSKCN0VV1QS.

"Darfur Conflict." *Thomson-Reuters Foundation News*. July 31, 2014, http://news.trust.org//spotlight/Darfur-conflict

Fisher, Jonah. "Myanmar's Rohingya: Truth, Lies and Aung San Suu Kyi." *BBC News*. January 27, 2017, www.bbc.com/news/world-asia-38756601.

Gallaway, Gloria, and Oliver Moore. "Turks Recall Envoy Over Harper's Remark." *Globe and Mail*. May 9, 2006, www.theglobeandmail.com/news/national/turks-recall-envoy-over-harpers-remark/article708646/.

Holt, Kate. "Nowhere to Run for the Children of South Sudan." *Al Jazeera*. December 15, 2016, www.aljazeera.com/indepth/inpictures/2016/12/run-children-south-sudan-161215045946302.html.

Jehl, Douglas. "Officials Told to Avoid Calling Rwanda Killings 'Genocide.'" *New York Times*. June 10, 1994, www.nytimes.com/1994/06/10/world/officials-told-to-avoid-calling-rwanda-killings-genocide.html.

Kessler, Glen, and Colum Lynch. "U.S. Calls Killings in Sudan Genocide." *Washington Post*. September 10, 2004, www.washingtonpost.com/wp-dyn/articles/A8364-2004Sep9.html.

Mathieu, Annie. "Leon Mugesera inculpé au Rwanda." *Le Soleil*. February 2, 2012, www.lapresse.ca/le-soleil/actualites/justice-et-faits-divers/201202/02/01-4491951-leon-mugesera-inculpe-au-rwanda.php. In French.

Mouradian, Khatchig. "'I Want for Armenians What I Want for Kurds:' An Interview with Mayor Abdullah Demirbas." *Armenian Weekly*. October 29, 2011, http://armenianweekly.com/2011/10/29/demirbas/.

Nebehay, Stephanie. "Time to Refer Syrian War Crimes
     to ICC: UN Inquiry." *Reuters*. February 18, 2013,
     www.reuters.com/article/us-syria-crisis-warcrimes-
     idUSBRE91H06920130218.

Nield, Richard. "Wau Displaced Tell of Death and Horrifying
     Escapes." *Al Jazeera*. December 21, 2016, www.aljazeera.
     com/indepth/features/2016/12/wau-displaced-death-
     horrifying-escapes-161220103833871.html.

Simons, Marlise, and Neil MacFarquhar. "Court Issues
     Arrest Warrant for Sudan's Leader." *New York Times*.
     March 4, 2009, www.nytimes.com/2009/03/05/world/
     africa/05court.html.

"The Triumph of Evil: 100 Days of Slaughter; A Chronology
     of U.S./UN Actions." *Frontline*. www.pbs.org/wgbh/
     pages/frontline/shows/evil/etc/slaughter.html.

"UN: 'Ethnic Cleansing Underway' in South Sudan."
     Al Jazeera. December 1, 2016, www.aljazeera.
     com/news/2016/12/ethnic-cleansing-south-
     sudan-161201042114805.html.

"Van Prepared as Restored Akhtamar Church to Re-open."
     Today's Zaman. March 28, 2007, www.todayszaman.
     com/national_van-prepared-as-restored-akhtamar-
     church-to-re-open_106626.html.

FILM

We Are All Rwandans. Directed by Debs Gardner-Paterson.
     2008. London, United Kingdom: Catsiye Productions.

GOVERNMENT SOURCES

"Recognition and Commemoration of Armenian Genocide."
Debates of the Senate (Hansard). 1st session, 37th
Parliament, Vol. 139, Issue 124, June 13, 2002,
www.parl.gc.ca/Content/Sen/Chamber/371/
Debates/124db_2002-06-13-e.htm#86.

N.G.O. REPORTS

"Public Document: Warrant of Arrest for Omar Hassan
Ahmad Al Bashir." March 4, 2009, https://www.icc-cpi.
int/CourtRecords/CR2009_01514.PDF.
"Report of OHCHR Mission to Bangladesh: Interviews with
Rohingyas Fleeing from Myanmar Since 9 October
2016." February 3, 2017, www.ohchr.org/Documents/
Countries/MM/FlashReport3Feb2017.pdf.
"UNHCR Global Appeal 2012–2013 — Chad." December 1,
2011, http://www.unhcr.org/4ec230faa.html.
"United Nations Report of the Commission of Inquiry on
Lebanon Pursuant to Human Rights Council Resolution
S–2/1." November 23, 2006, p. 18, www.refworld.org/
docid/45c30b6e0.html.

SPEECHES

Clinton, Bill. "Remarks to the People of Rwanda." Speech at
the Miller Center. Kigali, March 25, 1998. https://www.
youtube.com/watch?v=ofAyKqyOKEM.

Index